Unleashing Innovation
Startups in India

Dr Surya Garg

TABLE OF CONTENTS

ACKNOWLEDGMENT

Dear Readers,

Welcome to "Unleashing Innovation: Startups in India," a comprehensive exploration of one of the most dynamic and exciting landscapes in the world—the Indian startup ecosystem. In this book, you'll embark on a journey through the triumphs, challenges, and inspiring stories that define India's entrepreneurial spirit.

India's startup ecosystem has witnessed remarkable growth, from the bustling streets of Bangalore to the thriving tech hubs of Mumbai and Delhi-NCR. It's a story of audacious dreamers who have dared to disrupt traditional industries, innovate relentlessly, and create solutions that impact millions.

Through this book, we aim to provide you with an insider's view of the Indian startup journey. Whether you're an aspiring entrepreneur, an investor seeking opportunities, a policy maker shaping the ecosystem, or simply someone curious about the exciting world of startups, there's something here for you.

Inside this book, you will:

Meet the Visionaries: Discover the profiles and journeys of influential Indian entrepreneurs who have transformed industries and redefined success.

Navigate Challenges: Delve into the complexities and hurdles that startups face on their path to growth and success, from regulatory challenges to funding constraints.

Explore Innovations: Gain insights into the cutting-edge technologies and trends that are propelling Indian startups forward, from artificial intelligence to sustainable practices.

Celebrate Impact: Explore the social enterprises and impact startups that are making a difference in India and beyond, addressing critical issues such as healthcare, education, and environmental sustainability.

Learn from Failures: Understand the valuable lessons learned from startup failures and how resilience plays a pivotal role in the entrepreneurial journey.

Glimpse the Future: Speculate on the future of startups in India, uncovering emerging sectors and opportunities that hold immense promise.

We've collaborated with industry experts, successful entrepreneurs, and thought leaders to bring you a well-rounded perspective on the Indian startup landscape. Our hope is that you'll find inspiration, valuable insights, and practical guidance within these pages as you embark on your own entrepreneurial adventures.

Thank you for choosing "Unleashing Innovation: Startups in India." We invite you to join us on this enlightening and transformative journey through the vibrant world of Indian startups.

Let's turn the page and explore the limitless possibilities together!

Warm regards,

Surya Garg
Author of "Unleashing Innovation: Startups in India"

Overview of the Indian Startup Ecosystem:

The Indian startup ecosystem has witnessed a remarkable transformation over the past few decades, evolving from a nascent landscape into a thriving hub of innovation and entrepreneurship. Today, it stands as one of the world's most dynamic and vibrant startup ecosystems, characterized by a confluence of factors that have propelled it to the global stage.

Historical Perspective:

The roots of India's startup ecosystem can be traced back to the early 1990s when economic liberalization policies began to open up the Indian market. This period marked the beginning of a new era, as it provided the freedom and opportunities for entrepreneurs to explore uncharted territories. However, it wasn't until the 2000s that the ecosystem began to gain significant traction.

Growth and Evolution:

The growth of India's startup ecosystem can be attributed to several key factors:

1. Demographic Dividend: India's youthful population has been a driving force, providing a vast talent pool of young, tech-savvy individuals eager to create and innovate.

2. Digital Revolution: The proliferation of the internet and mobile technology has democratized access to information and markets, allowing startups to reach a global audience.

3. Investor Confidence: The influx of venture capital firms, angel investors, and strategic investors has provided startups with the necessary capital to scale and grow.

4. Government Support: The Indian government launched the "Startup India" initiative in 2016, offering incentives, tax benefits, and ease of doing business for startups.

5. Entrepreneurial Spirit: Indian entrepreneurs have displayed remarkable resilience, adaptability, and the willingness to take calculated risks, which are essential qualities for startup success.

Key Milestones:

Several key milestones have marked the evolution of the Indian startup ecosystem:

1. Early Pioneers: Companies like Infosys and Wipro laid the groundwork for the IT industry in India, inspiring a new generation of entrepreneurs.

2. E-commerce Revolution: The emergence of e-commerce giants like Flipkart and Snapdeal in the early 2000s disrupted traditional retail and showcased the potential of online business models.

3. Tech Boom: The proliferation of tech startups in cities like Bangalore, often referred to as the "Silicon Valley of India," has contributed significantly to India's startup growth.

4. Unicorn Explosion: India has seen the rise of numerous unicorns (startups valued at over $1 billion), including Ola, Paytm, Byju's, and Zomato, cementing its status as a global startup hub.

5. Global Recognition: Indian startups have gained international recognition, with many expanding operations globally and attracting investments from overseas.

The Indian startup ecosystem is a testament to the power of innovation, resilience, and collaboration. It continues to evolve, with new sectors, technologies, and entrepreneurs constantly pushing the boundaries of what's possible. In the following chapters, we will delve deeper into various facets of this ecosystem, exploring success stories, challenges, innovations, and the roadmap ahead.

CHAPTER 1
THE INDIAN STARTUP LANDSCAPE

To understand the historical context and key milestones of the Indian startup ecosystem, it's important to recognize the significant developments that have shaped its growth over the years. Here's a chronological overview:

Historical Context (Pre-2000s):

1) Economic Liberalization (1991): India's economic liberalization policies in the early 1990s marked a pivotal moment. These reforms opened up the Indian economy to globalization, reduced trade barriers, and allowed foreign direct investment (FDI). This laid the groundwork for a more favorable environment for entrepreneurship.

    Early Years (2000s):

2) Dot-Com Era (Late 1990s - Early 2000s): The late 1990s and early 2000s witnessed the emergence of the internet and technology startups. Companies like Rediff.com, IndiaInfoLine, and Sify entered the online space.

3) E-commerce Pioneers (2000s): Online shopping

gained momentum with the establishment of e-commerce platforms. Companies like eBay India (2000) and MakeMyTrip (2000) introduced Indians to online retail and travel bookings.

Emergence of E-commerce (2007 - 2010s):

4) Flipkart's Founding (2007): Flipkart, founded by Sachin Bansal and Binny Bansal, marked the beginning of a new era in Indian e-commerce. It started as an online bookstore but expanded into a multi-category marketplace.

5) Rise of Other E-commerce Giants: Snapdeal (2010), Paytm (2010), and others joined the e-commerce race, diversifying product offerings and attracting significant investments.

Venture Capital Influx (2010s):

6) Increasing VC Investments: The Indian startup ecosystem witnessed a surge in venture capital investments during the 2010s. Venture capital firms and angel investors showed growing interest in India's startups.

Rise of Tech Startups (2010s):

7) Technology and Innovation: The 2010s saw a proliferation of tech startups across sectors such as fintech, healthtech, edtech, and more. Mobile technology and the app economy played a significant role in this growth.

8) Unicorn Boom: India saw the rise of numerous unicorns (startups valued at over $1 billion) during this period. Notable examples include Ola, Paytm,

Byju's, Zomato, and OYO.

Government Initiatives (2016 - Present):

9) tartup India (2016): The Indian government launched the "Startup India" initiative in 2016 to support and nurture startups. It offers incentives, tax benefits, and ease of doing business for startups.

Current Landscape (2020s):

10) Diverse Sectors: The Indian startup ecosystem diversified beyond e-commerce and technology into sectors like healthcare, agriculture, and sustainability.

11) Global Expansion: Indian startups have expanded their operations globally, attracting investments from overseas and establishing a global presence.

12) Investor Confidence: India continues to attract investment from both domestic and international venture capital firms, corporate investors, and sovereign wealth funds.

13) Innovation Hubs: Cities like Bangalore, Mumbai, Delhi-NCR, and Hyderabad have emerged as innovation hubs, hosting numerous startups, incubators, and accelerators.

These milestones represent key moments in the evolution of the Indian startup landscape. They showcase the resilience and innovation of entrepreneurs, growing investor confidence, and the transformative impact of technology on various sectors of the economy. The Indian startup ecosystem continues to thrive and adapt, creating opportunities for innovation and growth.

The rise of startups in India can be attributed to a combination of factors that have created a conducive environment for entrepreneurship and innovation. These factors have played a significant role in fostering the growth of the Indian startup ecosystem:

1. Demographic Dividend: India boasts a youthful population with a median age of around 28 years. This demographic dividend provides a vast talent pool of young, tech-savvy individuals who are eager to create and innovate.

2. Economic Liberalization: Economic reforms in the early 1990s opened up India's economy to globalization and reduced bureaucratic hurdles. This liberalization allowed for increased foreign investment and business opportunities.

3. Digital Transformation: The proliferation of the internet and mobile technology has transformed how businesses operate and connect with consumers. India's growing internet penetration has created new markets and opportunities for digital startups.

4. Investor Confidence: Venture capital firms, angel investors, and private equity firms have shown increasing interest in Indian startups. Their investments provide startups with the necessary capital to scale and grow.

5. Government Initiatives: The Indian government launched the "Startup India" initiative in 2016, offering incentives, tax benefits, and ease of doing business for startups. Various state governments have also introduced startup-friendly policies and incentives.

6. Innovation and Technology: India has a strong technical and engineering talent pool. The country's startup

ecosystem has leveraged emerging technologies such as artificial intelligence, machine learning, blockchain, and IoT to create innovative solutions.

7. Entrepreneurial Spirit: Indian entrepreneurs have displayed remarkable resilience, adaptability, and the willingness to take calculated risks. The success stories of early startups have inspired a new generation of founders.
8. Globalization: The trend of outsourcing and offshoring work to India has fueled demand for technology and innovation. Indian startups have capitalized on this trend, providing outsourcing services as well as innovative products.

9. Startup Support Ecosystem: Incubators, accelerators, and co-working spaces have proliferated across Indian cities, providing startups with mentorship, resources, and networking opportunities.

10. Educational Institutions: Top-notch engineering and business schools in India produce a steady stream of entrepreneurial talent. These institutions foster innovation and entrepreneurship through various programs and initiatives.

11. Market Size: India's large and diverse market of over a billion people offers startups a unique testing ground and a substantial customer base.

12. Global Recognition: Indian startups have gained international recognition, with many expanding their operations globally and attracting investments from overseas.

13. Collaboration and Networking: Startup communities and networking events, both online and offline, have facilitated collaboration and knowledge-sharing among

entrepreneurs.

These factors, combined with a dynamic and rapidly evolving business environment, have contributed to the exponential growth of startups in India. The Indian startup ecosystem continues to attract attention and investment on a global scale, making it a key player in the global innovation landscape.

CHAPTER 2
ENTREPRENEURIAL SUCCESS STORIES

Certainly, here are profiles and case studies of successful Indian startups and their founders:

1) Flipkart:
   a) Founders: Sachin Bansal and Binny Bansal
   b) Overview: Flipkart, founded in 2007, is one of India's leading e-commerce platforms. It started as an online bookstore and expanded into a diverse online marketplace. The company's success story includes overcoming logistical challenges, securing substantial investments, and pioneering innovations like cash-on-delivery.
   c) Key Milestone: Flipkart's acquisition by Walmart in 2018 for $16 billion remains one of the largest e-commerce acquisitions globally.

2) Ola:
   a) Founder: Bhavish Aggarwal
   b) Overview: Ola, founded in 2010, is India's largest ride-sharing platform. Bhavish Aggarwal's journey involved fierce competition with Uber, developing innovative solutions like Ola Auto and Ola Electric, and contributing to the Indian mobility revolution.

c)   Key Milestone: Ola's Electric Mobility division is making significant strides in the electric vehicle (EV) space, including the production of electric scooters.

3)   Paytm:
a)   Founder: Vijay Shekhar Sharma
b)   Overview: Paytm, founded in 2010, started as a mobile recharge and bill payment platform. It later expanded into digital wallets, online payments, and financial services. Vijay Shekhar Sharma's vision led to Paytm becoming one of India's leading fintech companies.
c)   Key Milestone: The successful launch of Paytm Payments Bank, which offers savings accounts, fixed deposits, and other banking services.

4)   Byju's:
a)   Founder: Byju Raveendran
b)   Overview: Byju's, founded in 2011, is India's largest edtech company. Byju Raveendran's innovative approach to personalized learning through technology revolutionized the education sector. The company offers a range of online learning programs and has expanded globally.
c)   Key Milestone: Becoming India's first edtech unicorn and securing significant investments to fuel global expansion.

5)   Zomato:
a)   Founders: Deepinder Goyal and Pankaj Chaddah
b)   Overview: Zomato, founded in 2008, is a leading online food delivery and restaurant discovery platform. The founders, Deepinder Goyal and Pankaj Chaddah, navigated challenges in the competitive food delivery market and expanded Zomato to numerous countries.

c) Key Milestone: Zomato's successful IPO in 2021, one of the largest in India's tech industry, marked a significant achievement.

6) Razorpay:
   a) Founders: Harshil Mathur and Shashank Kumar
   b) Overview: Razorpay, founded in 2013, is a fintech company that offers payment solutions to businesses. Harshil Mathur and Shashank Kumar's journey involved overcoming regulatory hurdles and building a comprehensive payments platform that empowers businesses.
   c) Key Milestone: Razorpay's rapid growth and funding rounds, showcasing its potential as a leading player in India's fintech industry.

7) OYO Rooms:
   a) Founder: Ritesh Agarwal
   b) Overview: OYO Rooms, founded in 2013 by Ritesh Agarwal, is India's largest hospitality chain, offering affordable and standardized accommodations. Ritesh's entrepreneurial journey began as a teenager when he started selling SIM cards. Today, OYO operates in numerous countries and is valued at billions of dollars.
   c) Key Milestone: Ritesh Agarwal's leadership and vision have propelled OYO to become a global hospitality brand, serving millions of travelers worldwide.

8) Udaan:
   a) Founders: Amod Malviya, Vaibhav Gupta, and Sujeet Kumar
   b) Overview: Udaan, founded in 2016, is a B2B e-commerce platform that connects manufacturers, wholesalers, traders, and retailers. Amod Malviya, Vaibhav Gupta, and Sujeet Kumar leveraged their

experience from Flipkart to build a platform addressing the complex supply chain needs of businesses.

c) Key Milestone: Udaan's rapid growth and ability to simplify business-to-business trade have made it a unicorn and a key player in India's e-commerce ecosystem.

9) Cure.fit:
   a) Founders: Mukesh Bansal and Ankit Nagori
   b) Overview: Cure.fit, co-founded by Mukesh Bansal (former Myntra CEO) and Ankit Nagori, is a health and fitness platform that offers a range of services, including fitness classes, healthy meals, and mental wellness programs. The startup has redefined health and wellness in India.
   c) Key Milestone: Cure.fit's innovative approach to holistic health, combining physical and mental well-being, has gained significant traction and funding.

10) Dream11:
   a) Founders: Harsh Jain and Bhavit Sheth
   b) Overview: Dream11, founded in 2008 by Harsh Jain and Bhavit Sheth, is a fantasy sports platform that allows users to create their fantasy teams for real-life sports events. The startup achieved remarkable growth by tapping into India's passion for cricket and sports.
   c) Key Milestone: Becoming India's first gaming unicorn and securing significant investments, including sponsorship deals with major sports leagues.

11) InMobi:
   a) Founder: Naveen Tewari
   b) Overview: InMobi, founded in 2007 by Naveen Tewari, is a global mobile advertising and

marketing platform. Naveen's vision led InMobi to become one of the pioneers in mobile advertising, serving brands and advertisers worldwide.

c) Key Milestone: InMobi's global reach and success in the competitive mobile advertising industry, with products like Glance and TruFactor.

12) Swiggy:
   a) Founders: Sriharsha Majety, Nandan Reddy, and Rahul Jaimini
   b) Overview: Swiggy, founded in 2014, is one of India's leading food delivery platforms. The founders, Sriharsha Majety, Nandan Reddy, and Rahul Jaimini, disrupted the food delivery industry by providing a convenient and efficient delivery service.
   c) Key Milestone: Swiggy's rapid expansion, innovative features like Swiggy Genie for deliveries beyond food, and its prominent position in India's online food delivery market.

13) Rivigo:
   a) Founders: Deepak Garg and Gazal Kalra
   b) Overview: Rivigo, founded in 2014 by Deepak Garg and Gazal Kalra, is a logistics technology company that focuses on improving the efficiency of trucking operations. The founders introduced the concept of relay trucking to optimize freight transportation.
   c) Key Milestone: Rivigo's innovative approach to logistics and its use of technology to create a more reliable and efficient trucking network.

14) Nykaa:
   a) Founder: Falguni Nayar
   b) Overview: Nykaa, founded by Falguni Nayar in 2012, is a leading online beauty and cosmetics

retailer in India. Falguni Nayar's vision was to provide a wide range of beauty products to Indian consumers through e-commerce.
c) Key Milestone: Nykaa's growth into a unicorn company, its successful IPO, and its role in transforming the beauty and cosmetics industry in India.

15) Freshworks:
a) Founder: Girish Mathrubootham and Shan Krishnasamy
b) Overview: Freshworks, co-founded by Girish Mathrubootham and Shan Krishnasamy in 2010, is a software-as-a-service (SaaS) company that provides customer engagement and support solutions. The founders disrupted the customer service software industry.
c) Key Milestone: Freshworks' global expansion, its portfolio of cloud-based software products, and its journey to becoming a successful SaaS unicorn.

16) PharmEasy:
a) Founders: Dharmil Sheth, Dhaval Shah, and Mikhil Innani
b) Overview: PharmEasy, founded in 2015, is a healthcare technology platform that facilitates medicine delivery and healthcare services. The founders aimed to simplify access to healthcare for consumers.
c) Key Milestone: PharmEasy's rapid growth, expansion into telemedicine, and its role in making healthcare more accessible and convenient.

17) BYJU'S:
a) Founder: Byju Raveendran
b) Overview: BYJU'S, founded by Byju Raveendran in 2008, is one of India's leading edtech platforms.

The startup offers personalized learning programs for students through its app, transforming the way education is delivered in India.

   c) Key Milestone: BYJU'S rapid growth, international expansion, and partnerships with educational institutions have made it a prominent player in the global edtech space.

18) PolicyBazaar:
   a) Founders: Yashish Dahiya, Alok Bansal, and Avaneesh Nirjar
   b) Overview: PolicyBazaar, founded in 2008, is India's largest online insurance aggregator. The founders, Yashish Dahiya, Alok Bansal, and Avaneesh Nirjar, disrupted the insurance industry by providing a platform for comparing and purchasing insurance policies online.
   c) Key Milestone: PolicyBazaar's significant market share and its role in promoting transparency and choice in the insurance sector.

19) Meesho:
   a) Founders: Vidit Aatrey and Sanjeev Barnwal
   b) Overview: Meesho, founded in 2015 by Vidit Aatrey and Sanjeev Barnwal, is a social commerce platform that enables individuals to start their own online businesses. It empowers entrepreneurs, especially women, to earn income through reselling products.
   c) Key Milestone: Meesho's growth as a platform for micro-entrepreneurs and its impact on job creation and economic empowerment.

20) Unacademy:
   a) Founders: Gaurav Munjal, Roman Saini, and Hemesh Singh
   b) Overview: Unacademy, founded in 2015, is a

prominent edtech platform that offers online courses and live classes. The founders, Gaurav Munjal, Roman Saini, and Hemesh Singh, created a platform that democratizes education access.

c) Key Milestone: Unacademy's rapid growth, a series of successful funding rounds, and its role in providing quality education to a wide audience.

21) Delhivery:
   a) Founders: Sahil Barua, Kapil Bharati, Mohit Tandon, Bhavesh Manglani, and Suraj Saharan
   b) Overview: Delhivery, founded in 2011, is a logistics and supply chain solutions company. The founders aimed to address challenges in the Indian logistics sector and built a tech-driven platform for e-commerce logistics.
   c) Key Milestone: Delhivery's extensive reach, last-mile delivery capabilities, and contributions to e-commerce growth in India.

22) Roposo:
   a) Founders: Mayank Bhangadia, Avinash Saxena, and Kaushal Shubhank
   b) Overview: Roposo, founded in 2012, is a social media platform that focuses on short video content. It gained popularity as an alternative to TikTok and has become a significant player in the short-video space.
   c) Key Milestone: Roposo's rapid user growth and acquisition by Glance, a subsidiary of InMobi.

23) Cred:
   a) Founder: Kunal Shah
   b) Overview: Cred, founded by Kunal Shah in 2018, is a fintech startup that rewards users for paying their credit card bills on time. Kunal Shah's unique approach to incentivizing financial responsibility

garnered significant attention.

c) Key Milestone: Cred's growth, successful funding rounds, and its role in promoting responsible credit card usage.

24) Cleartax:
   a) Founders: Archit Gupta, Raja Ram Gupta, and Srivatsan Chari
   b) Overview: Cleartax, founded in 2011, is an online tax filing and investment platform. The founders, Archit Gupta, Raja Ram Gupta, and Srivatsan Chari, aimed to simplify tax compliance for individuals and businesses.
   c) Key Milestone: Cleartax's role in simplifying tax filing and expanding into financial services.

25) InShorts (formerly News in Shorts):
   a) Founders: Azhar Iqubal, Anunay Arunav, and Deepit Purkayastha
   b) Overview: InShorts, founded in 2013, is a news aggregation and summarization app that provides concise news updates. The founders created a platform for busy readers seeking quick and relevant news.
   c) Key Milestone: InShorts' growth in the digital news space and its ability to deliver news in 60 words or less.

26) Toppr:
   a) Founder: Zishaan Hayath and Hemanth Goteti
   b) Overview: Toppr, founded in 2013, is an edtech platform that offers personalized learning for students. The founders, Zishaan Hayath and Hemanth Goteti, aimed to help students excel in exams through technology-driven solutions.
   c) Key Milestone: Toppr's expansion and its focus on personalized learning through AI-powered tools.

27) Cars24:
   a)   Founders: Vikram Chopra, Mehul Agrawal, Gajendra Jangid, and Ruchit Agarwal
   b)   Overview: Cars24, founded in 2015, is an online marketplace for buying and selling used cars. The founders disrupted the traditional used car market by providing transparency and convenience.
   c)   Key Milestone: Cars24's rapid growth and funding rounds, establishing itself as a leading player in the pre-owned car market.

These case studies represent a diverse range of startups across various sectors, including social media, fintech, tax, news aggregation, edtech, and automotive. The founders' innovative approaches and commitment to solving specific problems have propelled these startups to success in India's entrepreneurial landscape.

The Reasons Behind Success

The success of these startups in India can be attributed to a combination of factors that contributed to their growth and impact. Here are some insights into what made these startups thrive:

1. Identifying Unmet Needs: Successful founders often start by identifying unmet needs or pain points in the market. They recognize areas where innovation can make a significant difference. For example, Byju's recognized the need for personalized online education, while Swiggy addressed the demand for convenient food delivery.

2. Technology and Innovation: Most successful startups leverage technology and innovation to disrupt traditional industries. They build user-friendly apps and platforms that offer convenience, efficiency, and better user experiences.

This approach was evident in companies like Flipkart, Ola, and Paytm.

3. User-Centric Approach: Customer-centricity is a common trait among thriving startups. They prioritize understanding their target audience's preferences and pain points and continually iterate their products or services based on user feedback. Meesho's focus on empowering micro-entrepreneurs is an example of this approach.

4. Execution and Scaling: Execution is crucial for startup success. Founders must have a clear plan and the ability to scale their operations rapidly. Startups like Zomato and OYO demonstrated effective scaling strategies.

5. Timing and Market Readiness: Timing is often critical. Successful startups enter the market when conditions are favorable for their solutions. For instance, the rise of the smartphone and increased internet penetration in India created opportunities for startups like InMobi and Roposo.

6. Disruption and Differentiation: Thriving startups often disrupt existing business models and offer something unique. They differentiate themselves from competitors by providing better solutions or addressing specific pain points. PolicyBazaar's online insurance aggregation disrupted the traditional insurance distribution model.

7. Founder Vision and Leadership: Strong founder leadership and vision are key factors. Founders who are passionate about their mission and can inspire their teams play a crucial role in a startup's success. Founders like Byju Raveendran, Bhavish Aggarwal, and Vijay Shekhar Sharma embody this quality.

8. Adaptability and Resilience: Startups often face challenges and setbacks. The ability to adapt to changing

circumstances and learn from failures is essential. Successful founders, such as those at Freshworks and PharmEasy, exhibit resilience and adaptability.

9. Investor Support: Access to funding and support from investors can significantly impact a startup's growth trajectory. Many successful startups attracted investments from venture capital firms and angel investors at crucial stages of their development.

10. Regulatory Compliance: Startups that navigate regulatory challenges effectively and ensure compliance with relevant laws can maintain their operations smoothly. This factor is particularly relevant in sectors like fintech, where regulatory compliance is stringent.

11. Team Building: Building a talented and dedicated team is vital. Founders must surround themselves with individuals who share their vision and can execute on it. The ability to attract and retain top talent is a competitive advantage.

12. Market Expansion: Successful startups often expand their operations beyond India's borders. They tap into global markets, leveraging their products or services' strengths. For example, Ola expanded to international markets like the UK and Australia.

These insights underscore the importance of a combination of factors, including innovation, user-centricity, execution, and leadership, in the success of startups in India. Thriving startups address market needs, provide innovative solutions, and adapt to evolving conditions to remain competitive and grow.

CHAPTER 3
CHALLENGES AND OBSTACLES

Indian startups, while thriving and achieving significant success, also face several challenges that can impact their growth and sustainability. Here's an examination of some of the key challenges faced by Indian startups:

1) Regulatory and Compliance Hurdles:
   a) Complex regulatory frameworks and bureaucratic red tape can pose challenges for startups, especially in sectors like fintech and healthcare.
   b) Frequent changes in tax policies and compliance requirements can create uncertainty and administrative burdens.

2) Access to Funding:
   a) While India has seen an increase in venture capital and angel investments, access to early-stage funding remains a challenge for many startups.
   b) Limited access to risk capital can hinder innovation and expansion plans.

3) Market Competition:
   a) Indian markets are highly competitive, with both domestic and international players vying for market share.

b) Startups need to differentiate themselves and continuously innovate to stay ahead.

4) Talent Acquisition and Retention:
   a) Attracting and retaining skilled talent is a significant challenge. Competition for top talent from established companies and global firms is fierce.
   b) Startups may struggle to offer competitive compensation and benefits packages.

5) Infrastructure and Logistics:
   a) Infrastructure challenges, including inadequate transportation networks and logistics systems, can affect supply chain efficiency and distribution.
   b) Improving last-mile connectivity remains a concern.

6) Digital Divide:
   a) Despite the growth of internet penetration, a significant digital divide still exists in India. Access to high-speed internet and digital literacy varies across regions.
   b) This divide can limit the customer base and access to online services.

7) Data Privacy and Security:
   a) Data privacy regulations, such as GDPR and India's own data protection laws, impose strict requirements on data handling.
   b) Compliance with these regulations and ensuring data security can be challenging for startups.

8) Scaling Operations:
   a) Scaling a startup's operations can be complex, especially in a diverse and vast market like India.
   b) Expanding to new cities or regions may require overcoming logistical challenges and adapting to

local nuances.

9) Funding Dependence on Foreign Investors:
   a) Many Indian startups rely heavily on foreign venture capital funding. Over-dependence on foreign investors can leave startups vulnerable to global economic conditions.

10) Market Volatility:
   a) Economic and market volatility, such as the impact of the COVID-19 pandemic, can disrupt operations and funding availability.
   b) Startups need to build resilience to navigate uncertain economic conditions.

11) Intellectual Property Protection:
   a) Protecting intellectual property can be challenging in India, with issues related to patent registration and trademark enforcement.
   b) Startups must invest in IP protection strategies.

12) Social and Cultural Challenges:
   a) Startups addressing sensitive issues, such as healthcare or social reform, may face resistance due to cultural norms and traditions.
   b) Building trust and overcoming societal challenges can take time.

13) Exit Opportunities:
   a) The Indian startup ecosystem is still evolving, and exit opportunities like acquisitions and IPOs are limited compared to more mature markets.
   b) Investors may face challenges in realizing returns on their investments.

Despite these challenges, Indian startups have demonstrated resilience and adaptability. They have leveraged their innovative ideas, entrepreneurial spirit, and a growing pool of skilled professionals to overcome obstacles and achieve remarkable success. The Indian government's initiatives, such as "Startup India," aim to address some of these challenges and create a more conducive environment for startups to thrive.

Specific Challenges

Indian startups face specific challenges related to regulations, funding, and market dynamics. Let's examine these hurdles in more detail:

Regulatory Hurdles:

1. Complex Regulatory Environment: India has a complex regulatory environment that can be challenging for startups to navigate. Regulations can vary by state and sector, leading to compliance complexities.

2. Taxation: Frequent changes in tax policies and the application of the Goods and Services Tax (GST) can create uncertainty and compliance burdens for startups.

3. Data Privacy and Security: Compliance with data privacy regulations, including India's proposed Personal Data Protection Bill, can be demanding. Startups must invest in data security measures and legal compliance.

4. Intellectual Property: Protecting intellectual property rights, such as patents and trademarks, can be costly and time-consuming. Enforcement of IP rights can also be challenging.

5. Foreign Investment Regulations: Certain sectors have restrictions on foreign investment, which can affect fundraising efforts and market entry for startups.

Funding Hurdles:

1. Early-Stage Funding: Access to early-stage funding, especially seed and angel investments, can be challenging for startups. Many investors prefer to invest in later-stage, more established startups.

2. Venture Capital Dominance: A significant portion of funding comes from venture capital firms. This reliance on VC funding can create pressure on startups to achieve rapid growth and profitability.

3. Valuation Expectations: Startups may face high valuation expectations from investors, which can be unrealistic given the market dynamics and early-stage revenue generation.

4. Limited IPO Opportunities: The Indian stock exchange has limited opportunities for startups to go public, compared to more mature markets like the United States.

Market-Specific Hurdles:

1. Intense Competition: The Indian market is highly competitive, with numerous startups competing for market share. This competition can make it challenging to stand out and achieve sustainable growth.

2. Diverse Consumer Base: India's diverse population and cultural nuances require startups to tailor their products and marketing strategies to various regions and demographics.

3. Infrastructure Challenges: Inadequate infrastructure, including transportation and logistics networks, can impact supply chain efficiency and distribution.

4. Digital Divide: Despite increasing internet penetration, a

significant digital divide still exists. Access to high-speed internet and digital literacy can vary widely across regions.

5. Consumer Behavior: Understanding and influencing consumer behavior in a diverse and dynamic market like India can be a significant challenge.

6. Economic Volatility: Economic and market volatility, such as the impact of the COVID-19 pandemic, can disrupt consumer spending patterns and affect startups' operations and funding availability.

Despite these hurdles, Indian startups have demonstrated resilience and adaptability. Many have successfully overcome regulatory challenges, secured funding, and found innovative ways to address market-specific complexities. Government initiatives, investor interest, and a growing pool of skilled talent continue to contribute to the growth of the Indian startup ecosystem.

Startups can overcome the regulatory, funding, and market-specific challenges in India through a combination of strategies and approaches. Here's how they can navigate these hurdles:

Regulatory Challenges:

1. Legal Expertise: Startups should seek legal counsel to understand and navigate the complex regulatory environment. Legal experts can help with compliance, contract negotiations, and intellectual property protection.

2. Compliance Measures: Implement robust compliance measures from the beginning to avoid legal issues later. Stay informed about changes in regulations and adapt your business practices accordingly.

3. Engage with Industry Associations: Join industry associations relevant to your sector. These associations often advocate for favorable regulations and can provide guidance on compliance.

4. Data Protection: Invest in data security and privacy measures to ensure compliance with data protection regulations. This includes securing user data and implementing GDPR-like practices.

5. Government Initiatives: Leverage government initiatives such as "Startup India" for support and incentives. These programs offer resources, mentorship, and financial benefits to startups.

Funding Challenges:

1. Bootstrapping: Consider bootstrapping initially by using personal savings or revenue generated from early customers. This can help you build a viable product or service before seeking external funding.

2. Angel Investors and Incubators: Connect with angel investors, incubators, and accelerators. These organizations can provide not only funding but also valuable mentorship and resources.

3. Venture Capital: When seeking venture capital, focus on building a strong pitch and business plan. Showcase your team's capabilities and your startup's growth potential.

4. Alternative Funding Sources: Explore alternative funding sources such as crowdfunding, strategic partnerships, and government grants.

5. Financial Prudence: Demonstrate financial prudence by managing expenses efficiently and having a clear plan for

the use of funds. Investors appreciate startups that can stretch their capital.

Market-Specific Challenges:

1. Market Research: Conduct thorough market research to understand your target audience's preferences, pain points, and behavior. Adapt your product or service accordingly.

2. Localization: Customize your offerings to cater to the diverse consumer base in India. Localization can include language, cultural, and regional considerations.

3. Partnerships: Collaborate with local partners who have a deep understanding of the market. Partnerships can help with distribution, marketing, and regulatory compliance.

4. Adaptation: Be flexible and willing to adapt your business model based on market feedback and changing conditions. Startups that pivot, when necessary, often fare better.

5. Digital Inclusion: Address the digital divide by considering low-bandwidth solutions and providing offline capabilities for users with limited internet access.
6. Economic Resilience: Build resilience by having contingency plans for economic downturns or market fluctuations. Diversify revenue streams if possible.
7. Customer-Centric Approach: Continuously engage with customers to gather feedback and improve your offerings. Customer satisfaction and loyalty are essential in a competitive market.
8. Scalability: Develop scalable processes and technologies that can support growth. Scaling efficiently can help you capture a larger market share.
Overcoming these challenges requires determination, adaptability, and a strong focus on your startup's mission. It's essential to build a resilient team, remain agile, and seek

mentorship from experienced entrepreneurs who have faced similar hurdles. Remember that challenges are a part of the entrepreneurial journey, and each obstacle presents an opportunity for learning and growth.

CHAPTER 4
FUNDING AND INVESTMENT LANDSCAPE

Analysis of funding sources for startups in India reveals a diverse landscape with various options available. Each funding source has its characteristics, advantages, and considerations:

1) Venture Capital (VC):
   a) Advantages: VCs provide substantial capital injections, mentorship, and networking opportunities. They typically invest in startups with high growth potential.
   b) Considerations: VCs often seek significant equity stakes and influence in the startup's decision-making. Startups should align their growth strategies with VC expectations.

2) Private Equity (PE):
   a) Advantages: PE firms invest in established startups looking to scale or mature companies. They bring expertise in scaling operations and offer growth capital.
   b) Considerations: PE investments are usually larger and come with stringent due diligence and reporting requirements. Startups should be

prepared for more in-depth scrutiny.

3) Angel Investors:
   a) Advantages: Angel investors provide early-stage funding, mentorship, and valuable industry connections. They often invest in innovative ideas and early-stage startups.
   b) Considerations: Angels typically seek equity or convertible debt in exchange for their investment. Personal relationships and pitch quality can significantly influence angel investment decisions.

4) Seed Funding:
   a) Advantages: Seed funding is crucial for product development, market testing, and initial operations. It helps startups validate their ideas and achieve early milestones.
   b) Considerations: Startups need a well-defined business plan and a compelling pitch to attract seed investors. Seed funding rounds may involve convertible notes or SAFEs.

5) Government Initiatives and Grants:
   a) Advantages: Government initiatives like "Startup India" offer incentives, tax benefits, and access to resources and mentorship. Grants can provide non-dilutive funding for specific projects.
   b) Considerations: Eligibility criteria, application processes, and compliance requirements vary by program. Startups must meet specific criteria to qualify.

6) rowdfunding:
   a) Advantages: Crowdfunding platforms allow startups to raise capital from a broad base of individual investors. It can generate early interest and validate market demand.

b) Considerations: Successful crowdfunding requires effective marketing and communication strategies. Startups should offer compelling rewards or equity-based incentives.

7) Strategic Partnerships:
a) Advantages: Partnering with established companies can provide funding, access to distribution channels, and industry expertise. It can accelerate market entry.
b) Considerations: Startups must identify mutually beneficial partnerships and navigate complex negotiation processes.

8) Debt Financing:
a) Advantages: Debt financing involves borrowing funds from banks or financial institutions. It can provide working capital without diluting equity.
b) Considerations: Debt financing carries the obligation of repayment with interest. Startups should assess their ability to service the debt.

9) Corporate Venture Capital (CVC):
a) Advantages: CVCs are venture arms of established corporations. They offer funding, strategic guidance, and potential partnerships.
b) Considerations: Startups should ensure alignment with the corporate investor's long-term goals and strategic interests.

10) Accelerators and Incubators:
a) Advantages: Accelerator and incubator programs provide funding, mentorship, and resources in exchange for equity. They offer structured support to early-stage startups.
b) Considerations: Startups should select programs aligned with their industry and growth stage.

Participation may involve relocation and a fixed timeline.

The choice of funding source depends on a startup's stage, industry, growth plans, and the trade-offs they are willing to make, such as equity ownership and control. A well-rounded funding strategy may involve a combination of these sources to secure the necessary capital and resources for growth. Additionally, startups should consider the regional and sector-specific dynamics that can influence funding availability and preferences in India.

Incubators, accelerators, and crowdfunding platforms play crucial roles in supporting startups by providing funding, mentorship, resources, and access to networks. Here's an overview of the roles each of these entities plays in the startup ecosystem:

Incubators:

1. Support Early-Stage Startups: Incubators primarily work with early-stage startups that are often in the ideation or prototype phase.

2. Physical Space: Many incubators offer physical office spaces and infrastructure, creating a conducive environment for startups to work and collaborate.

3. Mentorship and Guidance: Incubators provide mentorship and guidance from experienced entrepreneurs and industry experts. This helps startups refine their business models and strategies.

4. Access to Funding: Some incubators provide seed funding or access to a network of angel investors or venture capitalists, allowing startups to secure their initial capital.

5. Training and Workshops: Incubators often conduct training sessions, workshops, and seminars on various aspects of entrepreneurship, including marketing, finance, and legal compliance.

6. Validation and Validation: By accepting a startup into their program, incubators validate the idea and business model, which can be attractive to future investors.

7. Duration: Incubation programs typically have a longer duration, ranging from a few months to a couple of years, depending on the incubator and the needs of the startup.

Accelerators:

1. Fast-Track Growth: Accelerators are designed to fast-track the growth of startups that already have a working product or prototype.

2. Intensive Programs: Accelerator programs are highly intensive and time-bound, usually lasting a few months. During this time, startups receive mentorship and resources to accelerate their growth.

3. Investment: Many accelerators provide seed funding or equity investment in exchange for a percentage of equity. This investment helps startups scale quickly.

4. Access to Networks: Accelerators offer access to a broad network of mentors, industry experts, and potential customers or partners. This network can be invaluable for market entry and business development.

5. Demo Days: Accelerator programs often culminate in a "Demo Day" where startups pitch their products or services to a room full of potential investors.

6. Focus on Execution: Accelerators place a strong emphasis on execution, helping startups refine their strategies, market positioning, and go-to-market plans.

Crowdfunding Platforms:

1. Diverse Funding Sources: Crowdfunding platforms allow startups to raise funds from a diverse pool of individual investors, often via online platforms.

2. Validation: A successful crowdfunding campaign can validate market demand and interest in a startup's product or service.

3. Early Customer Engagement: Crowdfunding backers are often early adopters and advocates who become early customers and help spread the word about the startup.

4. Access to Capital: Crowdfunding can provide startups with capital without the need to give up equity, making it an attractive option for early-stage financing.

5. Marketing and Exposure: Crowdfunding campaigns can generate media attention and exposure, helping startups build their brand and reach a broader audience.

6. Rewards or Equity-Based Crowdfunding: Startups can choose between rewards-based crowdfunding (where backers receive products or perks) or equity-based crowdfunding (where backers receive shares in the company).

7. Regulatory Considerations: Startups must comply with regulatory requirements when conducting crowdfunding campaigns, including legal and tax obligations.

Overall, incubators, accelerators, and crowdfunding

platforms serve as valuable resources for startups at different stages of development. Choosing the right program or platform depends on the startup's specific needs, goals, and stage of growth. Many successful startups have benefited from the support and resources provided by these entities to achieve rapid growth and success in the market.

CHAPTER 5
TECHNOLOGY AND INNOVATION TRENDS

Emerging technologies, including artificial intelligence (AI), blockchain, the Internet of Things (IoT), and others, are having a profound impact on various industries and are significantly shaping the future of businesses and societies. Here's an overview of the roles and impacts of these technologies:

1) Artificial Intelligence (AI):

   a) Role: AI encompasses machine learning, natural language processing, and computer vision. Its role is to enable machines to mimic human-like intelligence, making them capable of tasks such as data analysis, decision-making, and problem-solving.
   b) Impact:
      i) Automation: AI automates repetitive and mundane tasks, increasing efficiency and reducing human error.
      ii) Data Analysis: AI processes vast amounts of data to extract valuable insights and patterns, aiding decision-making.

    iii) Personalization: AI powers recommendation engines and personalization in various industries, enhancing user experiences.

    iv) Healthcare: AI improves disease diagnosis, drug discovery, and patient care through predictive analytics.

    v) Autonomous Systems: AI enables autonomous vehicles, drones, and robotics.

    vi) Customer Service: Chatbots and virtual assistants enhance customer support and engagement.

2) Blockchain:

a) Blockchain is a distributed ledger technology that provides a secure and transparent way to record and verify transactions without the need for intermediaries.

b) Impact:

    i) Decentralization: Blockchain reduces the need for central authorities and intermediaries in various industries.

    ii) Transparency: It enhances transparency and trust by providing a tamper-resistant ledger.

    iii) Supply Chain: Blockchain improves supply chain transparency, traceability, and efficiency.

    iv) Finance: Cryptocurrencies and smart contracts are built on blockchain, revolutionizing finance and payments.

    v) Identity Verification: Blockchain can be used for secure identity verification and management.

3) Internet of Things (IoT):

a) Role: IoT connects physical devices and objects to the internet, enabling them to collect and exchange data.

b) Impact:
- i) Smart Homes: IoT devices enhance home automation, security, and energy management.
- ii) Industrial IoT (IIoT): In industries, IoT improves operational efficiency, predictive maintenance, and asset tracking.
- iii) Healthcare: IoT enables remote patient monitoring, wearable devices, and healthcare data analytics.
- iv) Smart Cities: IoT is used for traffic management, waste management, and environmental monitoring.
- v) Agriculture: IoT aids precision agriculture, optimizing resource usage and crop yields.

4) 5G Technology:

a) Role: 5G is the fifth generation of wireless technology, offering faster speeds, lower latency, and increased connectivity.

b) Impact:
- i) Enhanced Connectivity: 5G enables faster internet speeds, leading to better streaming, gaming, and real-time applications.
- ii) IoT Acceleration: 5G facilitates the growth of IoT by connecting a massive number of devices simultaneously.
- iii) Autonomous Vehicles: 5G is essential for reliable vehicle-to-vehicle communication and autonomous driving.
- iv) Telemedicine: It supports high-quality video conferencing and remote healthcare services.
- v) Industry 4.0: 5G drives the adoption of smart factories and advanced manufacturing processes.

5) Augmented Reality (AR) and Virtual Reality (VR):
   a) Role: AR overlays digital information onto the physical world, while VR immerses users in entirely digital environments.
   b) Impact
      i) Training and Simulation: AR and VR are used for employee training, education, and simulation.
      ii) Gaming and Entertainment: VR provides immersive gaming experiences, while AR enhances marketing and entertainment.
      iii) Healthcare: AR assists in surgery planning and medical education, while VR aids in pain management and therapy.
      iv) Architecture and Design: Architects use AR for visualizing designs, and VR offers virtual property tours.
      v) Retail: AR enhances shopping experiences with virtual try-ons and product visualization.

These emerging technologies are transforming industries, improving efficiencies, and opening up new opportunities for innovation. However, they also bring challenges, including ethical considerations, data privacy concerns, and the need for regulations to ensure responsible use. As these technologies continue to evolve, their impact on businesses, societies, and daily life is expected to grow significantly.

CHAPTER 6
STARTUP HUBS AND CITIES IN INDIA

India has several major startup hubs that have played a significant role in fostering innovation, entrepreneurship, and economic growth. Here's an overview of some of the major startup hubs in India:

1) Bengaluru (Bangalore):
   a) Known as the "Silicon Valley of India," Bengaluru is the country's leading startup hub.
   b) Home to numerous tech parks, incubators, accelerators, and coworking spaces.
   c) A thriving ecosystem in sectors like IT, software development, e-commerce, biotechnology, and fintech.
   d) Houses major tech giants and research institutions, attracting talent and investments.

2) Delhi-NCR (National Capital Region):
   a) Delhi-NCR includes Delhi and its surrounding areas like Gurugram (Gurgaon) and Noida.
   b) Focused on e-commerce, edtech, fintech, and healthcare startups.
   c) Access to government institutions and corporate networks due to its proximity to the capital city.

3) Mumbai:
   a) Mumbai is a financial and entertainment capital with a growing startup ecosystem.
   b) Key sectors include fintech, media and entertainment, real estate tech, and health tech.
   c) Presence of venture capital firms, angel investors, and corporate accelerators.

4) Hyderabad:
   a) Known for its biotech and pharmaceutical industries, Hyderabad has a thriving startup ecosystem.
   b) Key sectors include life sciences, IT, aerospace, and gaming.
   c) Home to T-Hub, one of India's largest incubators.

5) Pune:
   a) Pune has a burgeoning startup scene driven by its strong IT and manufacturing sectors.
   b) Key areas include automotive tech, software development, and health tech.
   c) Access to a skilled workforce from top engineering colleges.

6) Chennai:
   a) Chennai's startup ecosystem focuses on areas like healthcare, manufacturing, and software development.
   b) Presence of several research institutions and universities.
   c) Upcoming hubs in OMR (Old Mahabalipuram Road) and Tidel Park.

7) Kolkata:
   a) Kolkata has seen a rise in technology startups and entrepreneurial activity.

b) Key sectors include e-commerce, logistics, and edtech.

c) Government initiatives to promote startups and innovation.

8) Pune:
   a) Pune has a burgeoning startup scene driven by its strong IT and manufacturing sectors.
   b) Key areas include automotive tech, software development, and health tech.
   c) Access to a skilled workforce from top engineering colleges.

9) Chandigarh-Tricity:
   a) Chandigarh and its neighboring towns are emerging as startup hubs in North India.
   b) Sectors include edtech, fintech, agritech, and healthcare.
   c) Government support through initiatives like the "Startup in Punjab" program.

10) Jaipur:
   a) Jaipur is making strides in the startup space with a focus on edtech, e-commerce, and tourism tech.
   b) The presence of incubators and accelerators has boosted the ecosystem.
   c) Access to a growing pool of tech-savvy talent.

These major startup hubs in India offer a diverse range of opportunities and resources for entrepreneurs. Each region has its unique strengths, industry focuses, and local advantages, making them attractive destinations for startups in various sectors. The government's "Startup India" initiative and increased investor interest have further fueled the growth of these startup ecosystems.

The prominence of major startup hubs in India can be

attributed to a combination of factors that create favorable environments for entrepreneurship and innovation. Here are some key factors contributing to their prominence:

1) Educational Institutions:
   a) Presence of top-tier universities and engineering colleges that produce a skilled talent pool.
   b) Collaboration between academia and startups for research and innovation.

2) Access to Capital:
   a) Availability of venture capital firms, angel investors, and seed funding networks.
   b) Attraction of foreign direct investment (FDI) and corporate investments.
   c) Government initiatives to promote startup funding.

3) Infrastructure:
   a) State-of-the-art technology parks, coworking spaces, and incubators.
   b) Robust IT infrastructure and reliable internet connectivity.

4) Industry Expertise:
   a) Concentration of industry-specific expertise and knowledge.
   b) Established clusters for specific sectors such as IT, biotech, and fintech.

5) Supportive Ecosystem:
   a) Presence of mentorship programs, accelerators, and incubators.
   b) Networking events, startup competitions, and hackathons to foster collaboration.

6) Government Initiatives:

a) "Startup India" and state-specific startup policies offering incentives and regulatory support.

b) Investment in infrastructure, skill development, and innovation programs.

7) Market Opportunities:
a) Access to a large and diverse domestic market with a growing middle class.
b) Opportunities for scaling and market testing within India.

8) Access to Talent:
a) Attraction of talent from across the country and abroad.
b) Easier recruitment due to the availability of a skilled workforce.

9) Industry Diversity:
a) Presence of startups in various industries, from technology and healthcare to e-commerce and fintech.
b) Opportunities for cross-industry collaboration.

10) Proximity to Investors:
a) Easy access to venture capitalists, angel investors, and corporate investors.
b) Increased visibility for startups among investors.

11) Cultural Factors:
a) A culture of entrepreneurship and risk-taking.
b) Encouragement of innovation and creativity.

12) Infrastructure Development:
a) Improvement in physical infrastructure, transportation, and logistics.
b) Proximity to major airports and ports for international connectivity.

13) Local Government Support:
    a) Supportive local governments that encourage startup growth.
    b) Easier regulatory processes and permissions for startups.

14) Successful Role Models:
    a) Presence of successful startups and entrepreneurs who inspire and mentor new ventures.

15) Networking Opportunities:
    a) Active startup communities and networking events.
    b) Access to industry associations and business networks.

These factors, combined with the entrepreneurial spirit and determination of founders, have contributed to the prominence of major startup hubs in India. They create dynamic ecosystems that foster innovation, facilitate growth, and provide the necessary resources for startups to thrive and succeed.

CHAPTER 7
GOVERNMENT INITIATIVES AND POLICIES

The Indian government has implemented several programs and policies to support startups and foster entrepreneurship. These initiatives aim to provide funding, mentorship, infrastructure, and regulatory support to create a conducive environment for startup growth. Here's a discussion of some of the key government programs and policies supporting startups in India:

1) Startup India:
   a) Objective: Launched in 2016, the Startup India initiative aims to promote and nurture startups across the country.
   b) Key Features:
      i) Simplified regulatory framework to ease business operations and reduce compliance burdens.
      ii) Tax benefits for eligible startups, including a three-year tax holiday and exemption from the "Angel Tax."
      iii) Access to funding through various government

schemes and funds.

    iv) Startup India Hub for networking, mentorship, and assistance in accessing resources.

    v) Intellectual Property Rights (IPR) support for patent filing and protection.

    vi) Special attention to women-led and rural startups.

2) Atal Innovation Mission (AIM):

    a) Objective: AIM aims to promote innovation and entrepreneurship among students, researchers, and startups.

    b) Key Features:

        i) Establishing Atal Tinkering Labs (ATLs) in schools to encourage innovation among students.

        ii) Atal Incubation Centers (AICs) to support startups in various sectors.

        iii) Atal New India Challenges (ANICs) to encourage startups to solve pressing societal problems.

        iv) Atal Community Innovation Centers (ACICs) to stimulate innovation at the community level.

3) Make in India:

    a) Objective: The Make in India program encourages the manufacturing and production of goods within the country, which can benefit startups in various industries.

    b) Key Features:

        i) Investment promotion and facilitation to attract foreign and domestic investments.

        ii) Easier business registration and land acquisition processes.

        iii) Focus on skill development and workforce enhancement to support manufacturing startups.

4) Digital India:
   a) Objective: The Digital India program aims to transform India into a digitally empowered society and knowledge economy.
   b) Key Features:
      i) Push for digital infrastructure development, including broadband connectivity.
      ii) Promoting digital literacy and e-governance.
      iii) Facilitating e-commerce growth, which benefits startups in the digital and tech sectors.

5) Pradhan Mantri Mudra Yojana (PMMY):
   a) Objective: PMMY provides financial support to micro-enterprises and small businesses, including startups, through loans.
   b) Key Features:
      i) Three categories of loans (Shishu, Kishor, and Tarun) based on the stage of business growth.
      ii) Collateral-free loans to promote entrepreneurship.
      iii) Encouraging banks and financial institutions to participate in funding startups.

6) Biotechnology Ignition Grant (BIG):
   a) Objective: BIG provides financial support to startups in the biotechnology sector.
   b) Key Features:
      i) Funding for proof-of-concept, prototype development, and validation.
      ii) Support for innovations and projects with potential societal impact.

7) Fund of Funds for Startups (FFS):
   a) Objective: FFS is an initiative to provide funding to startups through various venture capital funds.
   b) Key Features:

> i) Co-investment by the government in startups with participating VCs.
>
> ii) Encouraging VCs to invest in early-stage startups across sectors.

These government programs and policies play a pivotal role in nurturing the Indian startup ecosystem. They provide essential financial and regulatory support, foster innovation, and create a favorable environment for entrepreneurs to start and scale their ventures. The combined impact of these initiatives has contributed to the rapid growth of the startup ecosystem in India.

Policy changes can have a significant impact on the startup ecosystem in India, influencing various aspects of entrepreneurship, innovation, and business operations. The effects of policy changes on startups can be both positive and negative, depending on the nature and intent of the policies. Here are some potential impacts of policy changes on startups:

Positive Impacts:

1. Ease of Doing Business: Policy changes aimed at simplifying regulatory processes and reducing bureaucratic hurdles can make it easier for startups to register and operate their businesses. This encourages more entrepreneurs to enter the market.

2. Access to Funding: Government policies that provide tax incentives, grants, and subsidies to startups can significantly enhance their access to funding, making it easier for them to secure capital for growth and innovation.

3. Innovation: Supportive policies can encourage innovation by providing incentives for research and development activities, patent filing, and technology adoption. This can lead to the creation of cutting-edge

products and services.

4. Job Creation: A thriving startup ecosystem, supported by favorable policies, can lead to job creation, helping reduce unemployment and contributing to economic growth.

5. Investor Confidence: Clear and consistent policies can boost investor confidence in the startup ecosystem, attracting both domestic and foreign investment. This can lead to more significant funding rounds for startups.

6. Global Competitiveness: Policies that promote exports and international expansion can help startups compete on a global scale, increasing their competitiveness and market reach.

Negative Impacts:

1. Regulatory Challenges: Frequent policy changes or unclear regulations can create uncertainty for startups, making it difficult for them to plan and operate their businesses effectively.

2. Compliance Costs: Stringent regulatory requirements can increase compliance costs for startups, diverting resources away from innovation and growth.

3. Taxation: Changes in tax policies, especially if they result in higher tax burdens, can put financial strain on startups, reducing their profitability and ability to reinvest in the business.

4. Funding Uncertainty: Policy changes that impact investment incentives or tax benefits for investors can reduce the availability of funding for startups, making it harder for them to raise capital.

5. Market Entry Barriers: Protectionist policies or trade restrictions can make it challenging for startups to enter international markets, limiting their growth opportunities.

6. Intellectual Property Rights: Policies that inadequately protect intellectual property or make it difficult to enforce patents and copyrights can hinder innovation and discourage investment.

The impact of policy changes on startups depends on various factors, including the specific policies, the maturity of the startup ecosystem, and the ability of startups to adapt to regulatory changes. A well-balanced and supportive policy environment is essential for nurturing a thriving startup ecosystem and ensuring that startups can innovate, grow, and contribute to the economy effectively. Continuous engagement between the government, industry stakeholders, and startups is crucial to developing and implementing policies that benefit all parties involved.

CHAPTER 8
E-COMMERCE AND CONSUMER TECH

The rise of e-commerce, food delivery, and consumer tech startups has transformed the way businesses operate and consumers engage with products and services. Here's an overview of the growth and impact of these sectors:

1) E-Commerce:

    a) Growth Factors:
        i) Increased Internet Penetration: The widespread availability of high-speed internet and smartphones has enabled more people to shop online.
        ii) Digital Payments: The adoption of digital payment methods and secure transactions has boosted consumer confidence in online shopping.
        iii) Wide Product Selection: E-commerce platforms offer a vast array of products, from electronics to fashion, making them convenient one-stop shops.
        iv) Convenience: The convenience of doorstep delivery, easy returns, and 24/7 shopping

appeals to consumers.

v) Discounts and Offers: E-commerce platforms frequently offer discounts, cashback, and loyalty programs, attracting price-conscious consumers.

b) Impact:
   i) Market Expansion: E-commerce has expanded market reach, allowing businesses to sell nationally and internationally.
   ii) Entrepreneurship: It has opened doors for entrepreneurs to start online businesses with lower upfront costs.
   iii) Job Creation: The sector has created jobs in logistics, warehousing, and customer support.
   iv) Digital Transformation: Traditional retailers have embraced e-commerce to stay competitive.
   v) Consumer Behavior: E-commerce has influenced shopping behaviors, driving the adoption of online-first strategies.

2) Food Delivery:

a) Growth Factors:
   i) Changing Lifestyles: Busier lifestyles and urbanization have increased demand for food delivery services.
   ii) Mobile Apps: User-friendly food delivery apps offer a seamless ordering experience.
   iii) Variety of Cuisines: Access to a wide range of cuisines and restaurants appeals to diverse tastes.
   iv) Contactless Delivery: During the COVID-19 pandemic, contactless delivery gained prominence.
   v) Affordable Options: Affordable pricing and

frequent discounts make food delivery accessible.

b) Impact:
   i) Restaurant Revenue: Food delivery platforms have boosted restaurant revenue and customer reach.
   ii) Gig Economy: The gig economy has thrived with opportunities for delivery partners.
   iii) Digital Payments: Increased adoption of digital payments has streamlined transactions.
   iv) Cloud Kitchens: The rise of cloud kitchens or virtual restaurants has disrupted traditional dining.
   v) Global Expansion: Food delivery platforms have expanded internationally.

3) Consumer Tech:

a) Growth Factors:
   i) Mobile Technology: Smartphone proliferation has driven the growth of consumer tech applications.
   ii) Digital Transformation: Businesses have adopted tech solutions to enhance customer experiences.
   iii) IoT and Wearables: IoT devices and wearables have become popular, influencing health and lifestyle tracking.
   iv) AI and Personalization: AI-powered apps provide personalized recommendations and services.
   v) Subscription Models: Subscription-based services offer convenience and ongoing value.

b) Impact:
   i) Lifestyle Enhancement: Consumer tech

    innovations have improved daily life through smart devices, apps, and services.

ii) Entrepreneurship: Tech startups have emerged across sectors, including healthtech, fintech, and edtech.

iii) Data Privacy: Concerns around data privacy and security have become more pronounced.

iv) Job Creation: The growth of consumer tech has created jobs in software development, data analysis, and customer support.

v) Global Reach: Many consumer tech startups have achieved international success.

While these sectors have experienced remarkable growth and have positively impacted various industries, they have also faced challenges, such as regulatory scrutiny, competition, and evolving consumer preferences. The ongoing evolution of technology and business models will continue to shape the future of e-commerce, food delivery, and consumer tech startups, offering new opportunities and disruptions.

The market dynamics and competition within the e-commerce, food delivery, and consumer tech sectors are characterized by several key factors and trends:

E-Commerce:

1. Intense Competition: E-commerce is highly competitive, with major players like Amazon, Flipkart, and Alibaba vying for market share. Competition often leads to price wars and innovative marketing strategies.

2. Market Consolidation: Larger e-commerce companies frequently acquire smaller startups to expand their offerings and reach new customer segments. This consolidation contributes to the competitive landscape.

3. Customer Loyalty: Building customer loyalty is crucial. Loyalty programs, subscription models, and personalized recommendations are used to retain and engage customers.

4. Logistics Innovation: Efficient logistics and last-mile delivery solutions are essential for success. Companies invest in technologies like drone delivery and automation to gain a competitive edge.

5. Global Expansion: E-commerce giants expand internationally to tap into emerging markets. Localization and adaptation to local consumer preferences are essential for success in different regions.

Food Delivery:

1. Fierce Competition: The food delivery market is highly competitive, with players like Uber Eats, DoorDash, and Grubhub competing for market share. Intense competition often results in aggressive marketing and discounting.

2. Restaurant Partnerships: Food delivery platforms collaborate with a wide range of restaurants to offer diverse menus. Exclusive partnerships and restaurant incentives can give platforms a competitive advantage.

3. Delivery Speed: Speedy and reliable delivery is a competitive differentiator. Companies invest in optimizing delivery routes and reducing delivery times.

4. Technology Innovation: Innovations like contactless delivery, AI-driven recommendations, and virtual kitchens (cloud kitchens) have become focal points for staying competitive.

5. Global Expansion: Food delivery companies seek

opportunities for international expansion, adapting their strategies to local preferences and market conditions.

Consumer Tech:

1. Innovation Race: The consumer tech sector is characterized by rapid innovation. Companies compete to introduce new features, devices, and services to attract and retain users.

2. Platform Dominance: Major tech companies aim for platform dominance, offering ecosystems of interconnected products and services. Examples include Apple's ecosystem and Amazon's Alexa ecosystem.

3. User Data: Access to user data is a competitive advantage. Companies use data-driven insights to enhance user experiences and target advertising effectively.

4. Privacy and Regulation: Heightened concerns about data privacy have led to increased regulation and scrutiny. Compliance with privacy laws and transparency practices can influence consumer trust.

5. Emerging Technologies: Companies invest in emerging technologies like augmented reality (AR), virtual reality (VR), artificial intelligence (AI), and the Internet of Things (IoT) to gain a competitive edge.

6. Startup Disruption: Consumer tech startups disrupt established players by introducing innovative solutions in areas like fintech, healthtech, and edtech.

In all three sectors, customer-centricity, convenience, and innovation are key drivers of competition. Companies that can effectively leverage technology, provide exceptional user experiences, and adapt to changing consumer preferences are more likely to thrive in these dynamic and competitive markets. Additionally, regulatory compliance, data security, and responsible business practices are increasingly important factors in maintaining a competitive edge and building trust with consumers.

CHAPTER 9
HEALTHCARE, EDTECH, AND AGRITECH

Examining Indian startups in sectors like healthcare, education technology (EdTech), and agriculture technology (AgriTech) reveals a vibrant ecosystem of innovation addressing pressing challenges and opportunities:

Healthcare Technology Startups (HealthTech):

1. Practo: An Indian HealthTech platform offering telemedicine services, appointment booking, and health records management. It has played a significant role in increasing healthcare accessibility.

2. PharmEasy: An online pharmacy and healthcare platform that enables users to order medicines, book diagnostic tests, and access health records.

3. Cure.fit: An integrated health and wellness platform that offers fitness, nutrition, and mental health services. It has gained popularity for its fitness app, Cult.fit.

4. Portea Medical: A home healthcare service provider offering a range of medical services, including home visits

by doctors, nursing care, and physiotherapy.

5. Niramai: A startup focused on early breast cancer detection using thermography and artificial intelligence, providing a non-invasive and cost-effective screening solution.

Education Technology Startups (EdTech):

1. BYJU'S: A leading EdTech unicorn offering interactive online learning materials, including video lessons and live classes, for school students.

2. Unacademy: An online learning platform providing a wide range of courses, including exam preparation, skill development, and professional development.

3. Toppr: An adaptive learning platform for K-12 students that personalizes learning based on individual strengths and weaknesses.

4. UpGrad: Offers online higher education and professional development programs in partnership with universities and industry experts.

5. WhiteHat Jr. (now part of BYJU'S): Focused on teaching coding to children, this startup gained attention for its coding classes for kids.

Agriculture Technology Startups (AgriTech):

1. Ninjacart: A B2B AgriTech platform that connects farmers directly with businesses and retailers, reducing wastage and ensuring better prices for farmers.

2. CropIn: A digital farm management platform that helps farmers make data-driven decisions, optimize crop yields,

and enhance farm productivity.

3. AgroStar: An AgriTech platform that provides farmers with agronomic advice, quality agri-inputs, and a marketplace for buying and selling farm products.

4. DeHaat: An AgriTech startup that offers a one-stop solution for farmers, including access to quality inputs, advisory services, and market linkages.

5. RML AgTech: Focused on precision agriculture, this startup uses data analytics and technology to help farmers make informed decisions and increase crop yields.

These Indian startups showcase the diversity and innovation within the healthcare, EdTech, and AgriTech sectors. They leverage cutting-edge technologies, such as artificial intelligence, data analytics, and mobile applications, to address critical challenges in these domains. Additionally, the COVID-19 pandemic accelerated the adoption of digital solutions in healthcare and education, further boosting the growth of these sectors in India. As the Indian startup ecosystem continues to evolve, these sectors are likely to see even more innovation and investment.

Indian startups in healthcare, education technology (EdTech), and agriculture technology (AgriTech) have had a significant impact on various societal issues, contributing to positive changes in access, affordability, sustainability, and overall well-being. Here's an overview of their impact on societal issues:

1) Healthcare Technology Startups (HealthTech):

   a) Increased Healthcare Access: HealthTech startups have made healthcare services more accessible to remote and underserved areas through telemedicine and online consultations. This has been particularly crucial during the COVID-19 pandemic.

b) Affordability: These startups have introduced cost-effective healthcare solutions, reducing the financial burden on patients. Patients can access affordable medicines, diagnostics, and consultations.

c) Health Awareness: HealthTech platforms offer health education and awareness programs, empowering individuals to make informed health choices and adopt preventive measures.

d) Early Detection: Innovations in diagnostic technologies and artificial intelligence have enabled early disease detection, improving treatment outcomes and reducing mortality rates.

2) Education Technology Startups (EdTech):

a) Equal Access to Quality Education: EdTech startups have democratized education by making quality learning materials and expert-led courses accessible to students across urban and rural areas.

b) Skill Development: These platforms offer skill-based courses and vocational training, addressing unemployment and enhancing employability.

c) Personalized Learning: Adaptive learning technologies cater to individual learning needs, ensuring that no student is left behind.

d) Teacher Empowerment: EdTech tools have empowered teachers with resources, training, and innovative teaching methods to enhance classroom experiences.

e) Lifelong Learning: EdTech encourages continuous learning and upskilling, supporting lifelong education and career advancement.

3) Agriculture Technology Startups (AgriTech):

a) Empowering Farmers: AgriTech startups provide farmers with information, market access, and technology to improve crop yields and income, addressing rural livelihood challenges.

b) Waste Reduction: Platforms like Ninjacart reduce food wastage by streamlining the supply chain, ensuring that produce reaches consumers efficiently.

c) Sustainability: AgriTech promotes sustainable farming practices, including precision agriculture, reducing the environmental impact of agriculture.

d) Financial Inclusion: Through Agri-Fintech solutions, farmers gain access to credit and financial services, reducing their dependency on informal lenders.

e) Food Security: By optimizing agriculture and ensuring a stable food supply chain, AgriTech contributes to national and global food security.

These startups have also played a crucial role during challenging times, such as the COVID-19 pandemic, by providing essential services, ensuring the continuity of education, and supporting healthcare infrastructure. Additionally, they have spurred innovation, entrepreneurship, and job creation, contributing to India's economic growth.

However, challenges like data privacy, regulatory compliance, and ensuring equitable access remain. Continued collaboration between startups, government agencies, and civil society can further amplify the societal impact of these innovative solutions.

CHAPTER 10
SOCIAL ENTERPRISES AND IMPACT STARTUPS

Indian startups with a focus on social impact and sustainability are playing a crucial role in addressing some of the country's most pressing challenges. Here's an exploration of several notable Indian startups in these domains:

1) Clean Energy and Sustainability:

   a) Solar Home Systems: Startups like Orb Energy and Mera Gao Power are providing affordable solar home systems to off-grid rural communities, reducing dependence on non-renewable energy sources and improving energy access.

   b) EV Charging Infrastructure: Companies like Ather Energy are promoting electric vehicles (EVs) by building a network of EV charging stations, reducing carbon emissions and air pollution.

2) Agricultural Sustainability:

   a) Ninjacart: This AgriTech startup connects farmers

directly with retailers, reducing food wastage, ensuring fair prices for farmers, and promoting sustainable agriculture.

b) AgroStar: Offering agronomy advice, quality agri-inputs, and market linkages, AgroStar empowers farmers to adopt sustainable farming practices and increase crop yields.

3) Healthcare Access:

a) Practo: Practo provides telemedicine services, making healthcare consultations more accessible, especially in rural and underserved areas.

b) Swasth Foundation: This nonprofit organization focuses on improving healthcare access for marginalized communities by providing affordable healthcare services and health education.

4) Education and Skill Development:

a) BYJU'S: A leading EdTech startup offering interactive online learning materials, increasing access to quality education across India.

b) Labournet: Labournet provides vocational training and employment support to empower youth and underserved communities with employable skills.

5) Waste Management and Recycling:

a) Karo Sambhav: This startup addresses electronic waste management and recycling, promoting responsible e-waste collection and recycling practices.

b) Saahas Zero Waste: Saahas Zero Waste focuses on waste management solutions, including waste segregation, recycling, and circular economy initiatives.

6) Sustainable Fashion and Apparel:

a) No Nasties: A sustainable fashion brand producing organic and fair trade clothing, emphasizing ethical manufacturing practices and environmental sustainability.

b) GoCoop: An online marketplace for handloom and handicraft products, connecting artisans directly with consumers to promote traditional craftsmanship and fair trade.

7) Impact Investment:

a) Unitus Ventures: A venture capital firm that invests in startups creating social and environmental impact across sectors like healthcare, education, and livelihoods.

8) Renewable Energy and Clean Tech:

a) Tata Power Solar: A subsidiary of Tata Power, this company focuses on solar power solutions, contributing to India's renewable energy goals and reducing carbon emissions.

b) Greenlight Planet: Known for its solar-powered home lighting solutions, Greenlight Planet improves energy access in rural and off-grid areas, reducing reliance on kerosene lamps.

These startups align with the global sustainability agenda

and are committed to making a positive social and environmental impact. They often collaborate with NGOs, government bodies, and impact investors to amplify their reach and achieve their mission of creating a more sustainable and equitable future for India.

Focus on Social Impact and Sustainability

Indian startups with a focus on social impact and sustainability play a crucial role in addressing a wide range of societal challenges. Here's how they contribute to solving these issues:

1. Clean Energy and Sustainability:

Reducing Carbon Emissions: Startups in clean energy and sustainability help reduce India's carbon emissions by promoting renewable energy sources such as solar power and electric vehicles (EVs).

Energy Access: They improve energy access, especially in remote and underserved areas, reducing reliance on non-renewable energy sources and enhancing the quality of life for communities.

Air Pollution Reduction: By promoting EVs and sustainable energy solutions, these startups contribute to reducing air pollution, a significant health and environmental concern in India.

2. Agricultural Sustainability:

Farmers' Income: AgriTech startups empower farmers by providing access to market linkages, fair prices, and agronomy advice, which increases their income and financial stability.

Sustainable Farming Practices: They promote sustainable farming practices, reducing chemical inputs, conserving resources, and ensuring long-term agricultural sustainability.

Food Security: Through efficient supply chains and reduced food wastage, these startups contribute to food security by ensuring a stable food supply.

3. Healthcare Access:

Rural and Underserved Communities: HealthTech startups and telemedicine services improve healthcare access for rural and underserved communities, reducing health disparities.

Affordability: They provide affordable healthcare services, reducing the financial burden on patients and increasing their ability to seek medical care when needed.

Preventive Healthcare: Health education and awareness programs offered by these startups empower individuals to adopt preventive healthcare measures, improving overall community health.

4. Education and Skill Development:

Quality Education: EdTech startups increase access to quality education, narrowing the education gap between urban and rural areas and improving overall literacy rates.

Employability: Skill development programs offered by these startups enhance employability, reducing unemployment rates and promoting economic growth.

Teacher Empowerment: EdTech tools empower teachers with resources and training, improving the quality of education and enhancing students' learning experiences.

5. Waste Management and Recycling:

Environmental Impact: Startups focused on waste management and recycling reduce the environmental impact of waste disposal by promoting responsible waste collection and recycling practices.

Circular Economy: They contribute to the circular economy by reusing and recycling materials, reducing the need for virgin resources and minimizing waste.

6. Sustainable Fashion and Apparel:

Ethical Manufacturing: Sustainable fashion startups emphasize ethical manufacturing practices, ensuring fair wages and safe working conditions for artisans and laborers.

Environmental Sustainability: They prioritize environmentally friendly materials and production processes, reducing the fashion industry's negative ecological impact.

7. Impact Investment:

Socially Responsible Investing: Impact investors like Unitus Ventures provide capital to startups that are dedicated to creating social and environmental impact, fostering a more sustainable investment ecosystem.

These startups, through their innovative approaches and commitment to social impact and sustainability, are instrumental in addressing India's pressing societal challenges, including energy access, education inequality, healthcare disparities, and environmental degradation. They demonstrate that businesses can be a force for positive change and contribute to building a more equitable and

CHAPTER 11
STARTUP CULTURE AND WORK ENVIRONMENT

Indian startups have developed a unique work culture and set of practices that distinguish them from traditional corporate environments. These characteristics reflect the dynamic and entrepreneurial nature of the startup ecosystem in India. Here are some key insights into the work culture and practices of Indian startups:

1. Flat Organizational Structure: Many Indian startups have flat hierarchies, encouraging open communication and collaboration among team members. Decision-making processes are often more decentralized, allowing employees to have a say in company directions.

2. Innovation and Creativity: Startups foster a culture of innovation and creativity, encouraging employees to think outside the box and come up with unique solutions to problems.

3. Flexible Work Arrangements: Startups often offer flexible work arrangements, including remote work options and flexible hours, to accommodate the diverse needs of their

employees.

4. Entrepreneurial Spirit: The entrepreneurial spirit is at the core of startup culture. Employees are encouraged to take ownership of their projects and contribute to the company's growth.

5. Cross-Functional Collaboration: Startups emphasize cross-functional collaboration, with teams working closely together to achieve common goals. This encourages employees to learn from each other and broaden their skill sets.

6. Fast-Paced Environment: The fast-paced nature of startups means that employees often work on multiple projects simultaneously and are expected to adapt quickly to changing circumstances.

7. Meritocracy: Startups tend to be meritocratic, valuing talent and performance over seniority. This can lead to rapid career progression for those who excel in their roles.

8. Employee Empowerment: Employees in startups often have a high degree of autonomy and are encouraged to take ownership of their work. This empowerment fosters a sense of responsibility and commitment.

9. Informal Dress Code: Startups typically have a more relaxed dress code, with employees often dressing casually rather than in formal attire.

10. Work-Life Integration: While startups demand hard work and dedication, they also promote work-life integration, acknowledging the importance of maintaining a healthy work-life balance.

11. Celebration of Diversity: Many Indian startups celebrate

diversity and inclusivity, welcoming individuals from various backgrounds and fostering a multicultural work environment.

12. Lean Operations: Startups often operate with lean teams and limited resources, which encourages employees to be resourceful and efficient in their work.

13. Learning and Development: Startups value continuous learning and provide opportunities for employees to develop new skills and gain experience in various areas.

14. Casual and Fun Atmosphere: Startups often have a casual and fun atmosphere in the workplace, with activities like team outings, game nights, and office celebrations.

15. Social Responsibility: Some startups incorporate social responsibility into their culture, engaging in initiatives like corporate social responsibility (CSR) projects or environmentally sustainable practices.

It's important to note that the startup culture can vary widely depending on the company's size, industry, and leadership style. While these insights provide a general overview of the work culture and practices in Indian startups, individual experiences may differ from one organization to another. Overall, the culture of Indian startups reflects the spirit of innovation, agility, and adaptability that defines the startup ecosystem in the country.

In Indian startups, innovation, diversity, and inclusivity play significant roles in shaping the culture, driving success, and fostering a dynamic work environment. Here's how each of these elements contributes to the startup ecosystem in India:

1. Innovation:

a. Problem-Solving: Indian startups are known for their problem-solving orientation. They identify challenges faced by individuals and businesses and create innovative solutions to address them. This culture of innovation drives entrepreneurship and promotes economic growth.

b. Technological Advancements: Technology is at the heart of many Indian startups. They leverage cutting-edge technologies like artificial intelligence, blockchain, and IoT to create products and services that are often disruptive and transformative.

c. Competitive Edge: Innovation gives startups a competitive edge in the market. They can enter established industries and carve out niches by introducing new business models and approaches.

d. Scalability: Scalability is a key goal for startups, and innovation is essential for achieving it. Innovative products or services can reach a broader audience and generate rapid growth.

e. Customer-Centric Approach: Many startups prioritize a customer-centric approach to innovation, continuously iterating their offerings based on customer feedback and evolving needs.

2. Diversity:

a. Diverse Talent Pool: Indian startups recognize the value of diversity in their teams. They hire individuals from various backgrounds, cultures, and experiences, fostering a rich and multidimensional talent pool.

b. Cross-Cultural Perspectives: Diversity brings cross-cultural perspectives to the workplace, enabling startups to better understand and serve diverse customer bases in India and globally.

c. Innovation Catalyst: Diverse teams tend to be more innovative, as they bring different viewpoints and problem-solving approaches to the table. This diversity of thought can lead to creative breakthroughs.

d. Inclusive Leadership: Inclusive leaders within startups promote diversity and create an environment where every team member feels valued and heard.

3. Inclusivity:

a. Equal Opportunity: Inclusivity in Indian startups ensures that all employees have equal opportunities to contribute and advance within the organization, regardless of their background, gender, or other characteristics.

b. Employee Well-Being: Startups often prioritize employee well-being and mental health, creating inclusive policies and practices to support work-life balance and mental well-being.

c. Non-Discrimination: Inclusivity promotes a culture of non-discrimination and zero tolerance for harassment, creating a safe and welcoming workplace for all.

d. Enhanced Creativity: Inclusive teams are more likely to be creative and innovative, as they draw from a wider pool of perspectives and experiences.

e. Social Responsibility: Many startups engage in social responsibility initiatives, reflecting their commitment to inclusivity and giving back to the communities they serve.

Overall, innovation, diversity, and inclusivity are not only important for the growth and success of Indian startups but also for the broader societal impact they aim to achieve. These elements are interconnected and mutually reinforcing, contributing to a dynamic and forward-thinking startup ecosystem in India. As startups continue to play a pivotal role in India's economic development, these values will likely remain central to their culture and operations.

CHAPTER 12
EXIT STRATEGIES AND ACQUISITIONS

Exit options for Indian startups, including Initial Public Offerings (IPOs) and acquisitions, are critical considerations as they determine how founders and investors can realize returns on their investments. Here's a discussion of these exit options in the context of Indian startups:

1. Initial Public Offering (IPO):

- An IPO is the process through which a startup becomes a publicly traded company by offering shares to the public through a stock exchange, such as the Bombay Stock Exchange (BSE) or the National Stock Exchange (NSE).

Advantages:

a. Access to Capital: Indian startups can raise significant capital through an IPO, enabling them to fund growth, expand operations, and invest in research and development.

b. Brand Visibility: Going public enhances the company's brand visibility and credibility in the market, which can attract more customers, partners, and opportunities.

c. Liquidity for Stakeholders: Founders and early investors can achieve liquidity by selling their shares to the public or institutional investors.

Challenges:

a. Regulatory Compliance: The Indian capital market has strict regulatory requirements, including financial reporting and disclosure obligations, which can be complex and time-consuming.

b. Market Volatility: Publicly traded stocks are subject to market fluctuations and investor sentiment, which can affect the company's valuation and share price.

c. Loss of Control: Going public often results in the dilution of founders' ownership and decision-making power.

2. Acquisition:

- Acquisition involves another company purchasing a startup, often for cash, stock, or a combination of both.

Advantages:

a. Quick Liquidity: Acquisitions provide a faster and more certain path to liquidity for founders and investors compared to an IPO.

b. Access to Resources: The acquiring company may offer access to additional resources, including distribution channels, customer bases, and industry expertise.

c. Risk Mitigation: Being part of a larger organization can

help mitigate risks associated with competition, market changes, and economic downturns.
Challenges:

a. Integration Complexity: Post-acquisition integration can be challenging, with potential cultural differences and operational issues.

b. Loss of Independence: Startups may lose their independence and entrepreneurial culture after an acquisition, affecting decision-making and innovation.

c. Valuation Negotiations: Determining the acquisition price and deal terms can be complex and require negotiation.

3. Secondary Sale or Private Equity Investment:

- In a secondary sale, founders and investors sell their shares to private equity firms, venture capital funds, or other private investors.

Advantages:

a. Partial Liquidity: Founders and investors can achieve partial liquidity while retaining ownership and control.

b. Flexible Terms: Negotiating terms in a private sale offers more flexibility compared to an IPO or acquisition.

Challenges:

a. Limited Capital: Secondary sales may not provide the same level of capital infusion as an IPO or acquisition.

b. Exit Timing: Timing a secondary sale can be challenging, as it depends on finding willing buyers in the private market.

4. Merger:

- Merging with another company involves the combination of operations to form a single entity.

Advantages:

a. Synergies: Mergers can create synergies by combining complementary resources and capabilities.

b. Market Positioning: The merged entity can enhance its market position, competitiveness, and growth potential.

Challenges:

a. Integration Complexity: Mergers often require complex integration efforts, including aligning cultures, systems, and operations.

b. Ownership Structure: Determining the ownership structure and leadership roles in the merged entity can be challenging.

The choice of exit strategy for Indian startups depends on several factors, including the company's goals, market conditions, regulatory considerations, and the preferences of founders and investors. Additionally, Indian startups often evaluate the timing and readiness for each exit option to maximize returns and achieve their long-term vision.

Notable Acquisition

The Indian startup ecosystem has witnessed several notable acquisition deals in various sectors. These acquisitions have often involved established companies acquiring startups to expand their offerings, gain access to innovative technology, and strengthen their market position. Here are some notable acquisition deals in the Indian startup ecosystem:

1) Flipkart's Acquisition of Myntra:
   In 2014, Flipkart, one of India's leading e-commerce platforms, acquired Myntra, an online fashion retailer. This acquisition allowed Flipkart to strengthen its presence in the fashion and apparel segment and compete effectively with international e-commerce giants.

2) Walmart's Acquisition of Flipkart:
   In 2018, Walmart, the American retail giant, acquired a majority stake in Flipkart for approximately $16 billion. This acquisition marked one of the largest e-commerce deals globally and aimed to leverage Flipkart's online retail expertise to compete with Amazon in the Indian market.

3) Ola's Acquisition of Foodpanda:
   In 2017, Indian ride-hailing company Ola acquired Foodpanda, a food delivery platform, to enter the food delivery market and diversify its services. The acquisition allowed Ola to compete with other food delivery giants like Swiggy and Zomato.

4) Swiggy's Acquisition of Scootsy:
   In 2018, Swiggy, a prominent food delivery platform in India, acquired Scootsy, a Mumbai-based food and beverage delivery service. This acquisition expanded Swiggy's reach in the Mumbai market and strengthened its delivery capabilities.

5) Reliance Industries' Acquisition of JioMart:
   Reliance Industries, one of India's largest conglomerates, expanded its digital commerce presence by launching JioMart, an e-commerce

platform. While not an acquisition in the traditional sense, it demonstrates how established players are entering the e-commerce space to compete with existing startups.

6) Byju's Acquisition Spree:
Byju's, an Indian edtech startup, has been actively acquiring other edtech companies to expand its product offerings and user base. Some notable acquisitions include the purchases of WhiteHat Jr., Aakash Educational Services, and Great Learning.

7) Paytm's Acquisition of FreeCharge:
In 2017, digital payments and financial services platform Paytm acquired FreeCharge, a mobile wallet and payments company. This acquisition aimed to strengthen Paytm's position in the digital payments market.

8) PhonePe's Acquisition of Zopper:
PhonePe, a digital payment and financial services platform, acquired Zopper Retail, an omnichannel point-of-sale and hyperlocal delivery platform, to enhance its merchant offerings.

9) Reliance's Acquisition of Haptik:
Reliance Jio acquired Haptik, an AI-based chatbot platform, to bolster its digital offerings and provide customer support services through chatbots.

10) Zomato's Acquisition of Uber Eats India:
In 2020, Zomato acquired Uber Eats India, marking its entry into the food delivery segment in India. This acquisition strengthened Zomato's position in the highly competitive food delivery market.

These are just a few examples of notable acquisition deals in the Indian startup ecosystem. India's growing startup landscape continues to attract interest from both domestic and international companies looking to invest, collaborate, or acquire startups to tap into the country's vibrant entrepreneurial culture and vast consumer base.

CHAPTER 13
INVESTOR PERSPECTIVES

Investment trends in India have evolved over the years, reflecting changes in the startup ecosystem, economic conditions, and investor preferences. As of my last knowledge update in September 2021, here are some investment trends that were prevalent in India:

1. Increased Foreign Direct Investment (FDI):
   - India continued to attract significant foreign investment, particularly in sectors like technology, e-commerce, and manufacturing. The government's efforts to liberalize FDI policies and improve the ease of doing business contributed to this trend.

2. Growth of Venture Capital (VC) and Private Equity (PE):
   - VC and PE funding in Indian startups remained robust. Investors, both domestic and international, showed a keen interest in early-stage and growth-stage companies across various sectors, including fintech, healthtech, edtech, and e-commerce.

3. Rise of Unicorn Startups:
   - India saw the emergence of several unicorn startups

(startups valued at over \$1 billion), indicating the growth potential and investor confidence in the Indian market. Some of these unicorns were in sectors like food delivery, fintech, and edtech.

4. Focus on HealthTech and EdTech:
   - The COVID-19 pandemic accelerated the adoption of digital health solutions and online education platforms. Investors directed significant capital into healthtech and edtech startups to support their growth and innovation.

5. Sustainability and ESG Investments:
   - Environmental, Social, and Governance (ESG) considerations gained prominence in investment decisions. Impact investing and sustainable business practices became key considerations for many investors.

6. AgriTech and Rural-focused Investments:
   - AgriTech startups received increased attention as investors recognized the potential for technology-driven solutions to address challenges in agriculture and rural areas. These startups aimed to improve farmers' livelihoods and enhance supply chain efficiency.

7. Government Initiatives:
   - The Indian government launched initiatives such as the Startup India program and Digital India, which aimed to foster entrepreneurship and digital transformation. These initiatives encouraged investment in the startup ecosystem.

8. Real Estate and Infrastructure Investment Trusts (REITs and InvITs):
   - The introduction of Real Estate Investment Trusts (REITs) and Infrastructure Investment Trusts (InvITs) provided new avenues for investment in real estate and infrastructure projects, offering attractive yields to investors.

9. Increased Cross-border Investments:
   - Indian startups and companies expanded their reach globally, attracting investments and partnerships from international entities. This trend highlighted India's growing significance in the global business landscape.

10. Maturing Startup Ecosystem:
   - India's startup ecosystem continued to mature, with more startups achieving scale and profitability. Investors showed a preference for startups with a clear path to profitability and sustainable business models.

Please note that the investment landscape is subject to rapid changes, and new trends may have emerged since my last update. It's essential to stay updated with the latest developments and consult with financial experts and industry reports for the most current information on investment trends in India.

CHAPTER 14
FUTURE TRENDS AND PREDICTIONS

While I cannot predict the future with certainty, I can offer some speculation on potential directions and trends in the Indian startup ecosystem based on historical patterns and emerging dynamics:

1. Continued Growth in Tech Startups:
  - India's tech startup landscape is expected to continue growing, with a focus on sectors like fintech, healthtech, edtech, and artificial intelligence. Increased smartphone penetration and digital adoption will drive innovation in these areas.

2. Rise of Tier 2 and 3 Cities:
  - Startups are likely to expand their presence beyond major metros, tapping into the vast consumer base in tier 2 and 3 cities. This geographical diversification will fuel the growth of hyperlocal and vernacular-focused startups.

3. Sustainable and Impact-Focused Startups:
  - Sustainability and social impact will become integral to startups' missions. More entrepreneurs will focus on addressing environmental, social, and governance (ESG)

challenges, attracting impact investors and conscious consumers.

4. Convergence of Technologies:
   - Startups will explore the convergence of technologies such as AI, IoT, blockchain, and 5G to create innovative solutions across industries, including healthcare, agriculture, and manufacturing.

5. Deeper Corporate Engagement:
   - Corporates will increasingly engage with startups through corporate venture capital (CVC), incubators, and accelerators. Collaborations and partnerships between startups and established companies will facilitate innovation.

6. Digital Health and Telemedicine:
   - The digital health and telemedicine sector will continue to evolve, offering convenient and accessible healthcare solutions. Regulatory support and increased healthcare awareness will drive growth.

7. Evolving Regulatory Environment:
   - The Indian government is likely to introduce policies and regulations that further support the startup ecosystem. Clearer regulatory frameworks for emerging technologies and data privacy may emerge.

8. E-commerce Expansion:
   - E-commerce, including online retail and food delivery, will remain competitive. Startups will innovate in logistics, supply chain, and last-mile delivery to enhance customer experience.

9. Fintech and Digital Payments Innovation:
   - Fintech startups will drive financial inclusion, offering digital banking, lending, and insurance services to

underserved populations. Digital payments will continue to replace cash transactions.

10. Education and Upskilling:
   - Edtech startups will play a vital role in education and upskilling, offering personalized and tech-driven learning solutions. Lifelong learning will become the norm.

11. AgriTech Advancements:
   - AgriTech startups will leverage data analytics, IoT, and AI to enhance crop yield, improve supply chains, and provide farmers with market access.

12. Clean Energy and Sustainability:
   - Startups in clean energy, renewable resources, and sustainability will gain prominence as India focuses on reducing its carbon footprint and addressing environmental challenges.

13. Focus on Cybersecurity:
   - With the increasing digitization of businesses, cybersecurity startups will work to protect data and systems from cyber threats, potentially in collaboration with government initiatives.

14. Global Expansion:
   - Indian startups will continue to expand globally, targeting international markets and attracting foreign investment. This globalization will further India's reputation as a hub for innovation.

15. Shift Toward Profitability:
   - Startups will face increasing pressure to demonstrate profitability and sustainable business models, leading to a focus on unit economics and operational efficiency.

It's important to note that the success of these trends will depend on various factors, including government policies, economic conditions, technological advancements, and global events. Entrepreneurs, investors, and policymakers will collectively shape the future of the Indian startup ecosystem, which is expected to remain vibrant and dynamic in the years ahead.

India's startup ecosystem continues to evolve, and several emerging sectors are poised to offer significant opportunities for entrepreneurs and investors. As of my last update in September 2021, here are some of the emerging sectors and opportunities in the Indian startup landscape:

1. AgriTech:
   - AgriTech startups are addressing challenges in agriculture, including improving crop yield, supply chain efficiency, and access to markets. Technologies like IoT, AI, and data analytics are being used to modernize farming practices.

2. Clean Energy and Sustainability:
   - Startups in clean energy, renewable resources, and sustainability are gaining traction as India focuses on reducing its carbon footprint. Solar energy, wind power, and waste management solutions present growth opportunities.

3. HealthTech:
   - The COVID-19 pandemic accelerated the adoption of digital health solutions. HealthTech startups are providing telemedicine, remote patient monitoring, and healthcare analytics services to meet the growing demand for healthcare innovation.

4. EdTech:
   - The education technology sector in India is witnessing significant growth. EdTech startups are offering online learning platforms, upskilling courses, and personalized

education solutions to cater to the diverse learning needs of students and professionals.

5. FinTech and InsurTech:
   - The FinTech and InsurTech sectors continue to evolve, with startups offering digital banking, payment solutions, insurance products, and wealth management services. Financial inclusion and digital payments are key focus areas.

6. SpaceTech:
   - India's space technology sector is attracting attention from startups and investors. Companies are exploring opportunities in satellite technology, space exploration, and satellite-based services.

7. Gaming and eSports:
   - The gaming and eSports industry is on the rise, driven by increased smartphone penetration and a growing gaming community. Startups are developing mobile games, gaming platforms, and eSports events.

8. Cybersecurity:
   - With the increasing digitization of businesses, cybersecurity startups are in demand. These startups focus on protecting data, networks, and systems from cyber threats.

9. Logistics and Supply Chain Tech:
   - Startups in logistics and supply chain technology are optimizing last-mile delivery, warehousing, and inventory management. E-commerce growth is fueling demand for innovative solutions.

10. Space Tourism:
   - Although in its infancy, space tourism is an emerging sector with potential opportunities. Indian entrepreneurs are exploring suborbital and orbital space tourism ventures.

11. Electric Vehicles (EVs):
    - The EV sector is gaining momentum in India as the government promotes electric mobility. Startups are developing electric vehicles, charging infrastructure, and battery technologies.

12. Personal Finance and Wealth Management:
    - Personal finance startups are helping individuals manage their money, invest, and plan for their financial future. Robo-advisors and investment platforms are becoming popular.

13. FoodTech:
    - FoodTech startups are innovating in food delivery, cloud kitchens, and sustainable food production. The pandemic boosted online food delivery services, and this trend is expected to continue.

14. Smart Cities and UrbanTech:
    - Smart city solutions, including IoT-based infrastructure and urban planning, are gaining importance as India urbanizes rapidly. Startups are working on smart mobility, waste management, and energy-efficient solutions.

15. Environment and ClimateTech:
    - Startups focused on environmental conservation and climate change mitigation are emerging. These companies offer solutions related to air quality monitoring, waste reduction, and carbon offsetting.

16. Blockchain and Cryptocurrency:
    - The blockchain and cryptocurrency space is gaining attention, with startups exploring applications beyond cryptocurrencies, such as supply chain transparency, digital identity, and more.

Please note that the startup ecosystem is dynamic, and new sectors may have emerged since my last update. Entrepreneurs and investors should conduct thorough market research and stay updated on industry trends to identify the most promising opportunities in the ever-evolving Indian startup landscape.

CHAPTER 15
SUPPORT ECOSYSTEM FOR STARTUPS

Startups in India have access to a wide range of resources, including networking events, co-working spaces, incubators, accelerators, and support organizations. These resources can play a crucial role in helping startups grow, gain visibility, and access mentorship and funding. Here's an overview of some key resources available to startups in India:

1. Networking Events:
   - TiE (The Indus Entrepreneurs): TiE is a global network of entrepreneurs and professionals that hosts networking events, mentoring sessions, and conferences to connect startups with experienced mentors and investors.
   - Startup Grind: Startup Grind is a global community of entrepreneurs that organizes regular meetups, fireside chats, and conferences to foster networking and knowledge-sharing among startup enthusiasts.
   - NASSCOM Product Conclave: NASSCOM's annual event brings together entrepreneurs, investors, and industry experts to discuss emerging trends and opportunities in the tech startup ecosystem.

2. Co-Working Spaces:
 - WeWork: WeWork has a significant presence in India, offering co-working spaces equipped with modern amenities, networking opportunities, and a vibrant community of startups and freelancers.
 - 91springboard: 91springboard is a co-working space provider with multiple locations across India, providing startups with flexible workspaces, networking events, and access to resources.

3. Incubators and Accelerators:
 - Indian Angel Network (IAN): IAN is one of India's largest angel investor networks and also operates an accelerator program, which provides mentorship, funding, and support to early-stage startups.
 - Y Combinator (YC): While not Indian-based, YC has accepted several Indian startups into its renowned accelerator program, providing access to Silicon Valley's ecosystem and investors.
 - IIM Ahmedabad's CIIE: The Center for Innovation, Incubation, and Entrepreneurship (CIIE) at IIM Ahmedabad supports early-stage startups with incubation programs, mentorship, and access to investors.

4. Support Organizations:
 - NASSCOM: The National Association of Software and Service Companies (NASSCOM) supports the IT and software services industry in India and provides resources, networking opportunities, and advocacy for startups.
 - Startup India: The Indian government's flagship initiative, Startup India, offers various incentives and support programs for startups, including access to funding, mentorship, and regulatory assistance.
 - YourStory: YourStory is a media platform that covers the Indian startup ecosystem and offers valuable insights, resources, and news for entrepreneurs.

5. Venture Capital and Angel Investor Networks:

- Sequoia Capital India: Sequoia Capital is one of the leading venture capital firms in India, providing funding and mentorship to startups.

- Accel Partners: Accel is another prominent venture capital firm with a strong presence in the Indian startup scene.

- Indian Angel Network (IAN): IAN, mentioned earlier, is a network of angel investors who often invest in and mentor startups.

6. Government Initiatives:

- MUDRA (Micro Units Development and Refinance Agency) Loan Scheme: This government scheme provides loans to micro and small enterprises, including startups, to support their growth.

- Make in India: The Make in India initiative aims to promote manufacturing and entrepreneurship in the country, offering various incentives and support for startups in manufacturing sectors.

These resources represent just a fraction of the support available to startups in India. It's essential for entrepreneurs to research and connect with the resources most relevant to their industry, stage, and goals. Building a strong network and leveraging these resources can significantly contribute to a startup's success in India's thriving ecosystem.

CHAPTER 16
LEGAL AND COMPLIANCE

Legal and compliance considerations are crucial for startups in India to ensure they operate within the framework of the law and avoid legal issues down the road. Here's an overview of some key legal and compliance considerations for startups in India:

1. Business Structure:
   - Choose an appropriate business structure, such as a sole proprietorship, partnership, limited liability partnership (LLP), private limited company, or one-person company (OPC), based on your business goals and liability preferences.

2. Business Registration:
   - Register your business entity with the relevant government authorities, such as the Registrar of Companies (RoC) for companies or the Ministry of Corporate Affairs (MCA) for LLPs.

3. Intellectual Property (IP) Protection:

- Protect your intellectual property, including trademarks, copyrights, patents, and trade secrets. File for trademark registration to safeguard your brand identity.

4. Taxation and GST:
- Comply with the Goods and Services Tax (GST) regime, if applicable, and ensure proper accounting and tax filings. Consider consulting with tax experts to optimize your tax structure.

5. Contracts and Agreements:
- Draft clear and legally binding contracts for employees, suppliers, customers, and partners. Contracts should define roles, responsibilities, payment terms, and dispute resolution mechanisms.

6. Funding and Securities Laws:
- If you plan to raise capital from investors, be aware of securities regulations and compliance requirements, including those related to private placements and venture capital funding.

7. Employment Laws:
- Comply with labor laws, including minimum wage requirements, employment contracts, and statutory benefits for employees. Be aware of anti-discrimination laws and workplace safety regulations.

8. Data Protection and Privacy:
- Ensure compliance with data protection laws such as the Personal Data Protection Bill, when enacted. Implement data protection policies and obtain consent for collecting and using personal data.

9. Regulatory Approvals:
- Depending on your industry, you may require licenses, permits, or approvals from sector-specific regulatory authorities. Verify and obtain the necessary clearances.

10. Environmental and Health Regulations:
   - If your business has environmental or health implications, ensure compliance with relevant laws and obtain necessary clearances, such as environmental impact assessments.

11. Compliance with Startup India:
   - Familiarize yourself with the incentives and benefits provided under the Startup India initiative, which includes compliance relaxation and tax benefits for eligible startups.

12. Accounting and Auditing:
   - Maintain accurate financial records and conduct regular audits as required by law. Compliance with the Companies Act and accounting standards is essential.

13. Contracts and IP Rights:
   - Ensure that contracts and agreements with employees, contractors, and vendors include clauses protecting your intellectual property rights.

14. Exit Strategy:
   - Plan your exit strategy carefully, whether it's through an acquisition, merger, or public offering. Legal considerations in exit negotiations are crucial.

15. Investor Agreements:
   - If you secure funding from investors, draft clear and comprehensive investment agreements, shareholder agreements, and term sheets to protect both your interests and those of your investors.

16. Compliance Calendar:
   - Create a compliance calendar to keep track of filing deadlines, statutory requirements, and renewal dates for licenses and permits.

17. Dispute Resolution:
   - Include dispute resolution clauses in contracts to specify the jurisdiction and mode of dispute resolution (arbitration, mediation, or litigation) in case conflicts arise.

18. Due Diligence:
   - When entering partnerships or investments, conduct due diligence on the legal and financial aspects of the entities involved.

It's advisable to work closely with legal and financial advisors who specialize in startup and business law to navigate these legal and compliance considerations effectively. Staying compliant with the law not only protects your business but also builds trust with stakeholders and potential investors.

Intellectual Property (IP), taxation, and regulatory frameworks are critical aspects of legal and compliance considerations for startups in India. Here's a detailed overview of each of these components:

1. Intellectual Property (IP):

   a. Trademarks: Register your brand name, logo, and other trademarks to protect your brand identity. Trademark registration in India is managed by the Controller General of Patents, Designs, and Trademarks.

   b. Copyrights: If your startup deals with creative content, software, or written materials, consider registering copyrights to protect your intellectual creations.

   c. Patents: If your startup develops unique inventions or processes, consider filing for patents with the Indian Patent

Office to protect your innovations.

d. Trade Secrets: Implement policies and contracts to safeguard trade secrets and confidential information within your organization.

e. IP Agreements: Draft agreements (e.g., non-disclosure agreements and licensing agreements) to manage IP rights, especially when collaborating with third parties or employees.

2. Taxation:

a. Goods and Services Tax (GST): Register for GST if your annual turnover exceeds the prescribed threshold. Comply with GST filing requirements and maintain proper records.

b. Income Tax: Be aware of income tax regulations for businesses, including corporate tax rates, deductions, and exemptions.

c. Withholding Tax: Understand withholding tax provisions, especially when making payments to foreign suppliers or service providers.

d. Transfer Pricing: Comply with transfer pricing regulations if your startup engages in cross-border transactions with related entities.

e. Angel Tax: Be mindful of the Angel Tax provisions, which may apply to the valuation of shares issued to investors.

f. Tax Deducted at Source (TDS): Ensure TDS compliance when making payments to employees, contractors, or vendors.

3. Regulatory Frameworks:

a. Company Law: Register your startup under the appropriate legal structure (e.g., private limited company, LLP) and adhere to the requirements of the Companies Act.

b. Foreign Direct Investment (FDI): Comply with FDI regulations and reporting requirements if your startup intends to raise funds from foreign investors.

c. Labor Laws: Ensure compliance with labor laws, including minimum wage, working hours, employee contracts, and social security contributions.

d. Data Protection: Prepare for data protection and privacy regulations, including compliance with the Personal Data Protection Bill (when enacted).

e. Environmental Regulations: If your startup has an environmental impact, obtain the necessary clearances and adhere to environmental regulations.

f. Industry-Specific Regulations: Be aware of and comply with industry-specific regulations that may apply to your business, such as food safety standards, pharmaceutical regulations, or financial services regulations.

g. Startup India Initiative: Leverage the benefits provided by the Startup India initiative, including compliance relaxation and tax incentives.

Navigating the legal and regulatory landscape in India can be complex, and it's advisable to seek legal and financial counsel to ensure compliance with all relevant laws and regulations. Non-compliance can result in legal consequences, financial penalties, and reputational damage, so it's essential to prioritize these considerations from the inception of your startup.

CHAPTER 17
MARKETING AND BRANDING STRATEGIES

Effective marketing and branding strategies are essential for startups to establish a strong presence in the market, attract customers, and build a brand identity. Here are some strategies that startups can consider:

1. Define Your Brand Identity:
   - Start by defining your brand's unique identity, values, and mission. Understand what sets your startup apart from competitors and communicate this clearly.

2. Target Audience Research:
   - Conduct thorough market research to identify your target audience's demographics, preferences, and pain points. Tailor your marketing efforts to resonate with your ideal customers.

3. Create a Strong Online Presence:
   - Develop a professional website that is mobile-responsive and user-friendly. Utilize social media platforms and online marketplaces relevant to your industry to reach a wider

audience.

4. Content Marketing:

- Create valuable and engaging content, such as blog posts, videos, infographics, and eBooks, to establish authority in your niche and attract organic traffic.

5. Search Engine Optimization (SEO):

- Optimize your website and content for search engines to improve visibility in search results. Focus on relevant keywords, meta tags, and high-quality backlinks.

6. Email Marketing:

- Build an email list and use email marketing campaigns to nurture leads, promote products or services, and provide valuable content to your subscribers.

7. Social Media Marketing:

- Choose the social media platforms where your target audience is active. Create a content calendar and engage with followers through regular posts, stories, and live sessions.

8. Influencer Marketing:

- Collaborate with influencers in your industry who have a significant following. Their endorsement can help you reach a larger and more engaged audience.

9. Paid Advertising:

- Invest in paid advertising campaigns, such as Google Ads, Facebook Ads, or sponsored content on relevant websites, to increase visibility and drive targeted traffic.

10. Public Relations (PR):

- Build relationships with journalists and media outlets to secure press coverage. Press releases and media mentions can boost credibility and brand awareness.

11. Networking and Partnerships:
   - Attend industry events, conferences, and meetups to network with potential customers, partners, and investors. Collaborate with complementary businesses for mutual benefit.

12. Customer Reviews and Testimonials:
   - Encourage satisfied customers to leave reviews and testimonials on your website and third-party review platforms. Positive feedback builds trust.

13. Referral Programs:
   - Create referral programs that incentivize existing customers to refer new ones. Offer discounts, rewards, or exclusive access in exchange for referrals.

14. Measure and Analyze:
   - Use analytics tools to track the performance of your marketing efforts. Monitor key metrics, such as website traffic, conversion rates, and ROI, and adjust your strategies accordingly.

15. Adapt and Evolve:
   - Stay flexible and be willing to adapt your marketing strategies based on data and changing market conditions. Experiment with new tactics to keep your approach fresh.

16. Build a Strong Brand:
   - Consistently communicate your brand message and values across all marketing channels. Your brand should evoke emotions and resonate with your audience.

17. Customer Engagement and Support:
   - Provide exceptional customer support and engage with your customers on social media and other platforms. Happy customers become brand advocates.

18. Storytelling:
   - Craft a compelling brand story that connects with your audience on a personal level. Share the journey, challenges, and successes that led to your startup's creation.

Remember that building a brand and achieving marketing success takes time and persistence. Continuously seek feedback from your customers and adapt your strategies to meet their needs and expectations. A well-executed marketing and branding strategy can help your startup stand out in a competitive market and establish a loyal customer base.

Successful Marketing Campaigns

Several Indian startups have executed successful marketing campaigns and achieved significant growth. Here are some notable marketing campaigns and case studies from Indian startups:

1. Ola's "Do Your Share" Campaign:
   - Ola, India's leading ride-sharing platform, launched the "Do Your Share" campaign to promote carpooling and reduce traffic congestion. The campaign encouraged users to share rides and contribute to a greener and less congested city. Ola provided incentives and discounts to carpooling users, resulting in increased adoption of the service.

2. Swiggy's "The Tummy Section" Campaign:
   - Swiggy, a popular food delivery platform in India, ran the "The Tummy Section" campaign to showcase its diverse food offerings. The campaign included creative advertisements and collaborations with food influencers to attract food lovers. Swiggy's witty and relatable marketing content resonated with its target audience, driving increased orders.

3. Zomato's "Food Ki Ruh" Campaign:
   - Zomato, another major player in the food delivery space, launched the "Food Ki Ruh" campaign, emphasizing its commitment to delivering food with care and hygiene. This campaign helped build trust with customers, especially during the COVID-19 pandemic, and highlighted the importance of food safety.

4. MakeMyTrip's "Dil Toh Roaming Hai" Campaign:
   - MakeMyTrip, a leading online travel booking platform, introduced the "Dil Toh Roaming Hai" campaign, encouraging people to fulfill their travel dreams. The campaign featured engaging videos showcasing different travel experiences and destinations, inspiring travelers to plan their trips through MakeMyTrip's platform.

5. Byju's "Fall in Love with Learning" Campaign:
   - Byju's, an edtech unicorn, launched the "Fall in Love with Learning" campaign, which focused on personalized and interactive learning experiences. Byju's used celebrity endorsements and engaging content to reach a wider audience, particularly parents and students. The campaign contributed to Byju's rapid growth and market leadership.

6. Paytm's "Scan & Pay" Campaign:
   - Paytm, a digital payments and financial services platform, promoted its "Scan & Pay" feature through a targeted marketing campaign. The campaign showcased the ease and convenience of cashless transactions, encouraging users to adopt digital payments.

7. PolicyBazaar's "Ullu Mat Bano" Campaign:
   - PolicyBazaar, an online insurance comparison platform, launched the "Ullu Mat Bano" campaign to raise awareness about the importance of informed insurance choices. The humorous and relatable campaign featured popular

comedian Kapil Sharma, helping PolicyBazaar gain brand recognition and trust.

8. PhonePe's "Karte Ja" Campaign:
  - PhonePe, a digital payment and financial technology company, introduced the "Karte Ja" campaign to promote its diverse range of services. The campaign emphasized the simplicity and convenience of using PhonePe for various financial transactions.

9. Nykaa's Content Marketing Strategy:
  - Nykaa, a beauty and skincare e-commerce platform, invested heavily in content marketing. Nykaa's blog and YouTube channel offer beauty tips, tutorials, and product reviews. This content-driven approach positioned Nykaa as a trusted source of beauty information and drove customer engagement.

These case studies highlight the diverse marketing strategies employed by Indian startups to engage their target audiences, build brand loyalty, and drive business growth. Successful campaigns often combine creativity, relatability, and an understanding of consumer needs and preferences.

CHAPTER 18
FAILURES AND LESSONS LEARNED

Analyzing startup failures in India can provide valuable lessons for aspiring entrepreneurs. While every failure has its unique circumstances, common themes and lessons can be derived from these experiences:

1. Lack of Market Research:
   - Many startups fail due to a lack of thorough market research. Entrepreneurs should invest time in understanding market trends, customer needs, and competition before launching their businesses. The lesson here is to validate your business idea and target audience thoroughly.

2. Insufficient Funding and Runway:
   - Inadequate capital and poor financial management often lead to startup failures. Entrepreneurs should secure enough funding to sustain operations, plan for contingencies, and have a clear financial roadmap. The lesson is to prioritize financial stability and plan for a longer runway.

3. Mismanagement of Funds:

- Misallocation of funds, overspending on marketing, and premature scaling are common financial mistakes that lead to failure. Startups should maintain strict financial discipline and allocate resources wisely.

4. Lack of a Strong Value Proposition:
   - Failing to offer a compelling value proposition can result in market rejection. Startups should focus on solving real customer problems and offering a unique value that differentiates them from competitors.

5. Poor Execution and Leadership:
   - Weak leadership, lack of execution, and poor decision-making can doom a startup. Founders should build a capable team, set clear goals, and lead by example. The lesson is to prioritize effective leadership and execution.

6. Ignoring Customer Feedback:
   - Ignoring customer feedback and failing to adapt to changing customer needs can lead to irrelevance. Successful startups actively seek and act on customer feedback to improve their products or services.

7. Scaling Too Quickly:
   - Premature scaling without a solid foundation can strain resources and lead to failure. Startups should focus on achieving product-market fit before scaling operations.

8. Regulatory and Compliance Issues:
   - Not understanding or complying with industry-specific regulations can lead to legal troubles and business disruption. Startups should prioritize compliance and seek legal advice when necessary.

9. Inadequate Marketing and Branding:
   - Failing to effectively market and build brand awareness can result in low customer acquisition. Startups should

invest in marketing and branding strategies that align with their target audience.

10. Lack of Adaptability:
    - Being rigid and resistant to change can be detrimental. Startups should remain agile, adapt to market dynamics, and pivot when necessary to stay relevant.

11. Weak Intellectual Property Protection:
    - Neglecting to protect intellectual property can lead to copycat competition. Startups should secure patents, trademarks, and copyrights as needed to safeguard their innovations.

12. Inadequate Networking and Partnerships:
    - Failing to build meaningful industry relationships and partnerships can limit growth opportunities. Entrepreneurs should actively network and explore collaboration opportunities.

13. Overreliance on a Single Revenue Stream:
    - Dependence on a single source of revenue can be risky. Diversify revenue streams to reduce vulnerability to market fluctuations.

14. Poor Customer Acquisition and Retention Strategies:
    - Not having a clear plan for customer acquisition and retention can hinder growth. Startups should develop effective strategies for acquiring and retaining customers.

15. Ignoring Cash Flow Management:
    - Focusing solely on revenue without considering cash flow management can lead to financial instability. Proper cash flow management is essential for sustaining operations.

16. Not Learning from Mistakes:
    - Failing to learn from past mistakes and repeat them is a

common pitfall. Entrepreneurs should have a growth mindset and continually learn from both successes and failures.

In summary, startup failures often stem from a combination of factors, including inadequate market research, financial mismanagement, poor leadership, and a lack of adaptability. Learning from these failures and applying the lessons learned can increase the chances of success for future entrepreneurial endeavors. It's important to view failure as an opportunity for growth and improvement.

Resilience and adaptability are two critical qualities for Indian startups, as they play a pivotal role in navigating the challenges and uncertainties of the business landscape. Here's why resilience and adaptability are essential:

1. Dynamic Market Conditions: India's business environment is characterized by rapid changes, evolving consumer preferences, and market volatility. Startups that can adapt quickly to changing market conditions are better positioned for success.

2. Regulatory Complexity: India has a complex regulatory landscape that can pose challenges to startups. Resilient startups can navigate these regulations effectively and adapt their business models to comply with legal requirements.

3. Economic Uncertainty: Economic fluctuations and global events can impact the stability of businesses. Resilient startups are better equipped to weather economic downturns and adapt their strategies to remain sustainable.

4. Competition: The Indian startup ecosystem is highly competitive. Startups that can adapt their products, services, and marketing strategies to stay ahead of competitors are more likely to thrive.

5. Customer Feedback: Customer preferences and expectations can change rapidly. Resilient startups actively seek and respond to customer feedback, making necessary adjustments to meet evolving needs.

6. Technological Advancements: Technology is constantly evolving, and startups must keep up with the latest advancements to remain competitive. Adaptability to new technologies is crucial for innovation and efficiency.

7. Funding Challenges: Raising capital can be challenging, and market conditions for funding can fluctuate. Resilient startups explore diverse funding sources and adapt their pitches and strategies to attract investors.

8. Globalization: Many Indian startups aim to expand internationally. Adaptability is essential when entering new markets, understanding local regulations, and tailoring products or services to meet international demand.

9. Pivot Potential: Startups may need to pivot their business models or strategies based on market feedback. Resilience enables founders to embrace change and make difficult decisions when necessary.

10. Employee Morale: Resilient leadership fosters a positive work culture, even during challenging times. This helps retain talent and maintain team morale, which is crucial for long-term success.

11. Learning from Failure: Resilient founders view failures as opportunities to learn and adapt. They are more likely to bounce back from setbacks and apply lessons to future endeavors.

12. Long-term Sustainability: Resilience and adaptability are

essential for the long-term sustainability of startups. They allow businesses to evolve, innovate, and remain relevant in the face of evolving market dynamics.

13. Customer Trust: Startups that consistently adapt to meet customer needs and provide value build trust and loyalty. This trust can lead to long-term customer relationships and word-of-mouth referrals.

In conclusion, the Indian startup ecosystem is both dynamic and challenging, making resilience and adaptability indispensable qualities for founders and their teams. Startups that can withstand adversity, embrace change, and continually adapt to evolving circumstances are better positioned to succeed and grow in the competitive Indian market.

CHAPTER 19
GLOBAL EXPANSION AND INDIAN STARTUPS ABROAD

The expansion of Indian startups into international markets has been a significant trend in recent years. Several factors have contributed to this phenomenon, and it reflects the growing ambition and global competitiveness of Indian entrepreneurs. Here's an exploration of Indian startups' expansion into international markets:

1. Market Saturation: As Indian markets become increasingly competitive and saturated, startups seek new growth opportunities abroad. Expanding internationally allows them to tap into larger customer bases and diversify their revenue streams.

2. Access to Funding: Indian startups have attracted significant investment from global venture capital firms and investors. With access to foreign capital, they have the financial resources to expand into international markets.

3. Technological Advancements: Indian startups, particularly in the tech sector, have developed cutting-edge technologies and solutions that are globally relevant. These

innovations can be applied to international markets with some customization.

4. Government Initiatives: Initiatives like the "Startup India" program have encouraged startups to think globally. The Indian government has also eased regulations for outward investments, making it easier for startups to expand abroad.

5. Indian Diaspora: The Indian diaspora, which is spread across the world, provides a valuable network for Indian startups looking to enter international markets. These connections can open doors for partnerships and collaborations.

6. Mobile Internet Penetration: India has one of the highest mobile internet penetration rates globally. Startups that have succeeded in the Indian market often have expertise in reaching mobile-first consumers, which can be applied in other emerging markets.

7. Niche Opportunities: Some Indian startups identify niche opportunities in international markets that align with their expertise. They enter these markets with specialized solutions and unique value propositions.

8. E-commerce and Cross-border Trade: E-commerce startups in India have leveraged cross-border trade to expand into international markets. Platforms like Amazon and Flipkart have facilitated global reach for Indian sellers.

9. Localization Efforts: Successful expansion requires startups to adapt their products, services, and marketing strategies to suit local preferences and cultures. Localization efforts are crucial for gaining acceptance in new markets.

10. Competitive Advantage: Indian startups often offer

cost-effective solutions compared to counterparts in Western countries. This competitive advantage can be a strong selling point in international markets.

11. Learning from Global Players: Indian startups have learned from global success stories like Google, Facebook, and Amazon. They aim to replicate aspects of these models in their own international expansion strategies.

12. Global Partnerships: Partnerships with international organizations, corporations, and investors provide startups with resources, market insights, and distribution channels to enter foreign markets.

13. Scaling Challenges: While expanding abroad offers growth opportunities, it also presents challenges such as regulatory compliance, cultural differences, and competitive landscapes. Startups must be prepared to address these challenges.

14. Brand Building: Building a strong and trusted brand is critical for success in international markets. Startups must invest in brand building and marketing efforts to establish credibility.

Indian startups that have successfully expanded internationally include companies like Zoho, Freshworks, OYO Rooms, and Byju's. Their experiences serve as valuable case studies for other Indian startups considering global expansion.

In conclusion, the expansion of Indian startups into international markets reflects the maturity and global ambition of the Indian startup ecosystem. With the right strategies, resources, and adaptability, Indian startups are well-positioned to compete on the global stage and contribute to India's reputation as a hub for innovation and entrepreneurship.

Indian startups expanding abroad have encountered both successes and challenges in their international endeavors. Here are some success stories and common challenges faced by Indian startups as they expand globally:

Success Stories:

1. Zoho Corporation: Zoho, a software development company, has expanded its operations to over 180 countries. They offer a suite of cloud-based applications and have gained global recognition for their customer-centric approach.

2. Freshworks: Freshworks, a customer engagement software company, has achieved significant success in international markets. They have a global customer base and offices in various countries, providing customer support, sales, and marketing solutions.

3. OYO Rooms: OYO, a hotel and hospitality startup, expanded its operations to multiple countries, becoming one of the largest hotel chains in the world. OYO's innovative business model and technology-driven approach have contributed to its global success.

4. BYJU'S: BYJU'S, an edtech startup, expanded into international markets, including the United States and the United Kingdom. Their adaptive learning platform has gained popularity among students worldwide.

Challenges Faced:

1. Market Adaptation: Adapting products or services to local market needs and preferences can be challenging. Cultural differences, regulatory requirements, and consumer

behavior must be carefully considered.

2. Competition: In international markets, Indian startups often face intense competition from well-established local and global competitors. Differentiating from existing players can be a significant challenge.

3. Regulatory Compliance: Navigating complex regulatory frameworks in foreign countries can be daunting. Startups must ensure compliance with local laws, data privacy regulations, and business licensing requirements.

4. Resource Allocation: Expanding abroad requires significant resources, including capital, talent, and time. Allocating these resources while maintaining operations in the home country can strain a startup's capabilities.

5. Localization: Effective localization of products, content, and marketing strategies is crucial for success. Ignoring local language and cultural nuances can hinder market penetration.

6. Talent Acquisition: Hiring and retaining talent in foreign markets can be challenging. Startups need access to a skilled workforce familiar with local conditions.

7. Brand Building: Building a brand presence in foreign markets takes time and investment. Startups may face skepticism from customers who are unfamiliar with their brand.

8. Financial Management: Managing currency fluctuations, foreign exchange risks, and financial reporting in multiple currencies can be complex and requires expertise.

9. Logistics and Supply Chain: Startups in sectors like e-commerce or logistics must address supply chain and

logistics challenges, including warehousing, transportation, and inventory management.

10. Customer Trust: Earning the trust of international customers can be a slow process. Offering excellent customer service and support is crucial for building trust.

Despite these challenges, Indian startups have demonstrated resilience and adaptability in expanding abroad. Successful expansion stories underscore the importance of thorough market research, strategic partnerships, and a customer-centric approach in overcoming international challenges.

In conclusion, Indian startups expanding abroad have the potential to achieve significant global success, but they must navigate numerous obstacles along the way. By learning from both successes and challenges, Indian startups can continue to make their mark on the global stage.

CHAPTER 20
ENTREPRENEURIAL ADVICE AND GUIDANCE

Successful Indian entrepreneurs and industry experts offer valuable tips and advice for aspiring entrepreneurs and startups. Here are some insights from their experiences:

1. Solve Real Problems:
   - Ritesh Agarwal, Founder of OYO: "Start with a problem you are truly passionate about solving. Passion is what will keep you going when things get tough."

2. Embrace Failure:
   - Kunal Bahl, Founder of Snapdeal: "Failure is a badge of honor. It means you risked failure. And if you don't risk failure, you will never innovate."

3. Focus on Customer Value:
   - N. R. Narayana Murthy, Co-founder of Infosys: "Customers are your best teachers. They will guide you to make your product better and better."

4. Stay Agile:
   - Naveen Tewari, Founder of InMobi: "Don't get too

attached to your own ideas. Be ready to pivot and change direction based on what you learn."

5. Build Strong Teams:
   - Binny Bansal, Co-founder of Flipkart: "Invest time and effort in building the right team. The right people can make or break your startup."

6. Persistence is Key:
   - Vijay Shekhar Sharma, Founder of Paytm: "Success is not about how you start, but how you finish. Keep at it and don't give up."

7. Adapt to Market Feedback:
   - Deep Kalra, Founder of MakeMyTrip: "Be ready to listen to your customers. They are the best source of insight into what's working and what's not."

8. Network and Learn:
   - Nikesh Arora, Chairman & CEO of Palo Alto Networks: "Networking is important. Meeting people, learning from them, and building relationships can open doors."

9. Focus on Quality:
   - Sundar Pichai, CEO of Google: "In the long term, you want to focus on quality. The rest takes care of itself."

10. Be Resilient:
   - Acharya Balkrishna, MD of Patanjali Ayurved: "Resilience is the ability to bounce back from failures and adversities. It's a crucial trait for entrepreneurs."

11. Stay Passionate:
   - Ratan Tata, Chairman Emeritus of Tata Sons: "I don't believe in taking the right decisions. I take decisions and then make them right."

12. Learn from Mistakes:
   - Shiv Nadar, Founder of HCL: "It's okay to make mistakes. The important thing is to learn from them and not repeat them."

13. Think Long-Term:
   - Mukesh Ambani, Chairman & MD of Reliance Industries: "In the journey of entrepreneurship, tenacity of purpose is supreme."

14. Embrace Technology:
   - Nandan Nilekani, Co-founder of Infosys: "Technology is a great enabler. It can transform industries and create new opportunities."

15. Have a Clear Vision:
   - Kiran Mazumdar-Shaw, Chairperson & MD of Biocon: "Your vision should be clear, concise, and compelling. It should inspire your team and stakeholders."

16. Build a Strong Culture:
   - Azim Premji, Chairman of Wipro: "Culture is the foundation of any successful company. It defines how things are done."

17. Stay Grounded:
   - Rahul Bajaj, Chairman of Bajaj Group: "Success should not go to your head, and failure should not go to your heart."

18. Give Back to Society:
   - N. R. Narayana Murthy, Co-founder of Infosys: "You must be the change you wish to see in the world."

These insights from successful Indian entrepreneurs and industry experts emphasize the importance of passion, adaptability, resilience, customer-centricity, and a continuous learning mindset in the entrepreneurial journey. It's essential for aspiring entrepreneurs to take these lessons to heart and apply them as they embark on their own startup journeys.

Aspiring founders looking to start their own businesses can benefit from guidance and insights from experienced entrepreneurs and industry experts. Here are some key pieces of guidance for aspiring founders:

1. Start with a Clear Problem: Identify a genuine problem or need in the market that your business can address. Successful startups are often born out of a desire to solve a real-world problem.

2. Passion and Commitment: Be passionate about your idea and committed to seeing it through. Entrepreneurship can be challenging, and your passion will be your driving force.

3. Validate Your Idea: Before investing significant time and resources, validate your business idea. Seek feedback from potential customers, conduct market research, and test your concept to ensure there's demand.

4. Build a Strong Team: Surround yourself with a capable and diverse team. Your team plays a crucial role in executing your vision and overcoming challenges.

5. Market Research: Understand your target market thoroughly. Know your competition, customer demographics, and market trends. This knowledge will inform your business strategy.

6. Business Plan: Develop a solid business plan that outlines your goals, target audience, revenue model, and marketing strategy. A well-structured plan is essential for attracting investors and guiding your operations.

7. Funding Strategy: Determine how you'll fund your startup. Options include bootstrapping, seeking investment from venture capitalists or angel investors, or exploring crowdfunding.

8. Embrace Technology: Leverage technology to streamline operations, reach a wider audience, and stay competitive. Stay updated on tech trends relevant to your industry.

9. Customer-Centric Approach: Put your customers at the center of your business. Listen to their feedback, iterate on your product or service, and build strong customer relationships.

10. Agility and Adaptability: Be prepared to pivot if your initial approach doesn't yield the desired results. Adapt to changing market conditions and customer needs.

11. Network: Build a strong professional network. Attend industry events, join entrepreneur organizations, and connect with mentors and advisors who can provide guidance and support.

12. Focus on Quality: Deliver high-quality products or services. Building a reputation for quality and reliability is crucial for long-term success.

13. Marketing and Branding: Develop a strong brand identity and marketing strategy. Effective marketing will help you reach and engage with your target audience.

14. Financial Management: Keep a close eye on your finances. Budget wisely, monitor cash flow, and plan for the financial sustainability of your business.

15. Resilience: Entrepreneurship often involves setbacks

and challenges. Develop resilience to bounce back from failures and keep moving forward.

16. Continuous Learning: Stay curious and keep learning. The business landscape evolves, and ongoing learning will help you adapt and innovate.

17. Legal and Compliance: Understand the legal and regulatory requirements for your industry and location. Comply with all relevant laws and regulations.

18. Give Back: Consider the social and environmental impact of your business. Explore opportunities to give back to the community or support sustainability initiatives.

19. Stay Grounded: Success can bring both praise and pressure. Stay humble, maintain work-life balance, and prioritize your well-being.

20. Measure Progress: Set clear metrics and key performance indicators (KPIs) to measure your startup's progress. Regularly assess whether you're meeting your goals.

Remember that entrepreneurship is a journey, and success often takes time. Be patient, stay focused, and keep learning from your experiences. Seek advice and mentorship from experienced entrepreneurs, and don't be afraid to seek help when needed. Your dedication and determination can lead to the growth and success of your startup.

CONCLUSION & OUTLOOK

In conclusion, the journey of entrepreneurship is marked by both opportunities and challenges. Here are some key takeaways for aspiring founders:

1. Start with Purpose: Begin your entrepreneurial journey with a clear purpose and a passion for solving real problems in the market.

2. Resilience Matters: Be prepared for setbacks and challenges. Resilience and the ability to bounce back from failures are crucial for long-term success.

3. Customer-Centric Approach: Put your customers at the forefront of your business. Continuously seek feedback and adapt your offerings to meet their needs.

4. Market Research: Thoroughly understand your target market, competition, and industry trends. Market research is the foundation of a successful business.

5. Team Building: Surround yourself with a capable and diverse team. Your team is instrumental in executing your vision.

6. Financial Prudence: Maintain sound financial management practices, including budgeting, cash flow monitoring, and long-term financial planning.

7. Adaptability: Be flexible and willing to pivot when necessary. Market dynamics change, and your ability to adapt can be a competitive advantage.

8. Networking: Build a strong professional network. Networking can open doors to valuable partnerships, mentorship, and growth opportunities.

9. Continuous Learning: Stay curious and committed to learning. Ongoing education and staying updated on industry trends are essential.

10. Brand and Marketing: Invest in building a strong brand identity and effective marketing strategies to reach and engage your target audience.

11. Legal and Compliance: Understand and comply with relevant legal and regulatory requirements to avoid potential pitfalls.

12. Social Responsibility: Consider the social and environmental impact of your business. Contributing to society and practicing sustainability can enhance your brand.

13. Give Back: As you achieve success, consider giving back to your community and supporting causes that align with your values.

14. Stay Grounded: Success can bring both praise and pressure. Maintain humility, prioritize work-life balance, and take care of your well-being.

15. Measurement and Progress: Set clear goals and metrics to measure your startup's progress. Regularly assess your performance against these benchmarks.

THE FUTURE OF STARTUPS IN INDIA

Entrepreneurship is a journey filled with opportunities for growth, innovation, and impact. It requires dedication, adaptability, and a willingness to learn from both successes and failures. By embracing these key takeaways and continually refining your approach, you can increase your chances of building a successful and sustainable business.

The future of startups in India appears promising and dynamic, characterized by both opportunities and challenges. Here's a reflection on the potential trajectory of startups in India:

1. Innovation and Technology: India has been witnessing a surge in technological innovation, particularly in areas like artificial intelligence, biotechnology, and fintech. As access to digital infrastructure expands, startups are likely to continue driving innovation and creating disruptive solutions.

2. Global Expansion: Indian startups are increasingly looking beyond domestic markets and expanding internationally. This trend is expected to continue as Indian entrepreneurs aim to tap into larger customer bases and diversify revenue streams.

3. Access to Capital: India's startup ecosystem has attracted significant investment from venture capitalists, private equity firms, and global tech giants. This access to capital is likely to fuel the growth of startups and support their scaling efforts.

4. Government Initiatives: Government initiatives like "Startup India" have created a conducive environment for entrepreneurship. Continued support from policymakers, including regulatory simplification and funding incentives,

can further boost the startup ecosystem.

5. Sector Diversity: Startups are emerging across a wide range of sectors, from e-commerce and healthtech to agritech and edtech. This diversification suggests that India's startup ecosystem is not limited to a single industry and has the potential to impact various aspects of the economy.

6. Impact on Job Creation: Startups have the potential to play a significant role in job creation in India. As these companies grow, they are likely to hire talent across various functions and contribute to reducing unemployment.

7. Challenges: Despite the opportunities, startups face challenges, including regulatory hurdles, intense competition, and access to skilled talent. Addressing these challenges will be crucial for sustained growth.

8. Sustainability and Social Impact: There is a growing emphasis on sustainability and social impact among Indian startups. Many founders are incorporating environmentally friendly practices and addressing societal issues through their businesses.

9. Collaboration: Collaboration between startups, established corporations, and academia is expected to increase. Such partnerships can foster innovation and create a supportive ecosystem for startups.

10. Learning from Failure: Indian entrepreneurs are increasingly embracing the concept of learning from failure. This mindset shift can lead to more resilient and adaptive startups in the future.

11. Investor Confidence: Investor confidence in the Indian startup ecosystem remains strong. Continued interest from

both domestic and international investors can provide startups with the necessary resources for growth.

12. Global Recognition: Indian startups are gaining global recognition for their innovation and entrepreneurship. This global presence can open doors to international partnerships and expansion opportunities.

In conclusion, the future of startups in India is marked by innovation, growth, and a commitment to addressing both business challenges and societal issues. While there will be obstacles along the way, the potential for startups to contribute to economic development, job creation, and technological advancement in India remains substantial. With the right support, entrepreneurial spirit, and a focus on sustainability, the Indian startup ecosystem is poised for continued success in the years to come.

REFERENCES & CITATIONS

The information and insights provided in this book are based on a wide range of publicly available sources.

Disclaimer: The information, insights & real-life examples provided in this book are for illustrative purposes only. Actual events and outcomes may vary.

For further insights and professional connections, Surya can be reached via email at **dr.suryagarg@gmail.com***. He welcomes engagement from like-minded professionals, aspiring entrepreneurs, and anyone keen on delving deeper into the dynamic world of startups.*